M000194176

THE WEAPONISATION
OF EVERYTHING

THE WEAPONISATION OF EVERYTHING

A FIELD GUIDE TO THE NEW WAY OF WAR

MARK GALEOTTI

YALE UNIVERSITY PRESS
NEW HAVEN AND LONDON

For information about this and other Yale University Press publications, please contact:
U.S. Office: sales.press@yale.edu   yalebooks.com
Europe Office: sales@yaleup.co.uk   yalebooks.co.uk

Set in Sabon MT by IDSUK (DataConnection) Ltd
Printed in Great Britain by TJ Books, Padstow, Cornwall

Library of Congress Control Number: 2021941543

ISBN 978-0-300-25344-3

A catalogue record for this book is available from the British Library.

10 9 8 7 6 5 4 3 2 1

To Anna, in the expectation that there will continue to be more swords than ploughshares around

Contents

Introduction

It's the day after tomorrow and, suddenly, the lights start going out. Trains coast to a stop on their tracks, factories on night shift grind to a halt and frustrated teenagers across the country wonder where the broadband has gone. It will later transpire that, for more than a year, hackers had carefully, professionally bypassed the seemingly impressive array of defences, backups and failsafes meant to secure the power grids supplying both eastern and western Japan. Electricity is still being generated in nuclear plants, wind turbines and old-fashioned fossil-fuel burners alike, but it simply isn't getting anywhere; the national grids are gridlocked. It will take forty-eight hours before the systems are finally cleared of the hostile malware and rebooted, two days in which everyone is reminded of their dependence on steady, plentiful and above all reliable power.

This is a largely bloodless attack, but not wholly so. There are fatalities in intensive care units where backup generators are not enough or are too slow to come online. Seventy-one people die in road accidents as traffic lights go dark. There is a litany of needless, trivial tragedies, as people fall down stairs in the sudden dark or, in one case, a man has a panic attack in a stuck lift in Osaka so severe that he kicks out the window and jumps to his death.

Who do you call in when it's a true national crisis? The military is deployed to deal with some of the secondary effects. One corollary casualty is its capacity to take part in the Keen Sword exercises the Japanese Self-Defence Forces had been about to stage with the US: soldiers are instead busy getting generators to care homes or helping the police patrol the streets against sporadic, opportunist looting.

The government quickly announces that this was an attack, even though it lacks a clear answer at first about how, let alone who. However, for months the public have been groomed, titillated or enraged by hostile media accounts of corruption and, in particular, mishandling of the national infrastructure. They are thus uncertain what to believe, and then decisively sway against the administration when hacked official emails are leaked, showing that ministers had been warned that a combination of legacy systems and penny-pinching updates risked catastrophic, cascading failures within the electricity grids. These emails are, worse yet, real. Spokespeople do their best to explain the context, that these warnings were offset by others which affirmed that the system was sturdy and 'fit for purpose', but this sounds weak and self-serving, especially as some of the other documents, it emerges, have been wiped from the government's systems.

It looks from the outside like a cover-up. The government's counter arguments are buried in a media feeding frenzy, stoked by suborned, genuinely outraged or simply opportunistic opinion-

formers, from politicians to TikTok stars. A video mocking the prime minister, who had unfortunately spoken beneath a campaign slogan reading 'the power to do good', goes viral, just as a picture of a photogenic young woman crying at the funeral of her 96-year-old grandfather – an ex-paramedic, who ran marathons for charity into his eighties – becomes the image of the aftermath. 'Was granddad not "fit for purpose", prime minister?' reads the headline in one tabloid.

Beijing had bid to replace the primary national grids of Japan two years back, although this had been disallowed on national security grounds. Now, a consortium 51 per cent owned by a Chinese power corporation makes a new offer, to rebuild the network with its own technology, at a bargain basement price, and at speed. The chairman of the parliamentary foreign affairs and defence committee had been one of the most trenchant critics of the original deal, but before he can comment, he is tragically killed in what the police conclude, for lack of any alternative evidence, was a bungled mugging. Others nonetheless still claim that this is all a complex ploy to win the contract and, with it, potentially gain control over the national grids. The consortium, though, includes a number of smaller Japanese companies which see their potential profits at risk. They, in turn, have sharp-toothed and well-paid lawyers on retainer, and a flurry of libel writs soon follows. Whether they are successful is arguably irrelevant: the potential cost of defending the cases prices many out of the battle and deters many more. People stop talking about the risks, at least in public.

Meanwhile, Beijing, while piously stating that it hopes 'Sinophobia' is not going to determine politics, deploys its big gun, offering the giant panda Chu Lin to the Ueno Zoological

Gardens in Tokyo. The deal goes through. And China gets a contract, a victory and, maybe, that long-term leverage it was looking for.

That is a nightmare scenario, a highly unlikely one, surely. But then again, so too was the idea that nineteen jihadists with boxcutters could hijack four airliners in the skies over the US in 2001 and carry out the deadliest terrorist attack in history. Or, for Iran, that a computer worm called Stuxnet, smuggled on a USB stick into the Natanz nuclear facility – buried deep underground, guarded by elite troops, anti-air systems and razor wire – could make the centrifuges it was using to enrich uranium for bombs rip themselves apart. Or that Russia could seize part of a neighbouring state in 2014 almost without any shots being fired, while claiming it was nothing to do with them. Each of the elements of the scenario, from infrastructure hacks to murders, has already been used in the undeclared shadow wars of the twenty-first century.

Weapons are getting more and more expensive, publics (even in authoritarian regimes) less and less tolerant of casualties and, anyway, the days when power was measured by coal mines, warm water ports and square kilometres of farmland are over. States have always used non-military means to bully, bait and beguile their way to victory. However, the world is now more complex and above all more inextricably interconnected than ever before. It used to be orthodoxy that interdependence stopped wars. In a way, it did – but the pressures that led to wars never went away, so instead interdependence became the new battleground. Wars without warfare, non-military conflicts fought with all kinds of other means, from subversion to sanctions, memes to murder, may be becoming the new normal.

4

In the process, the lines between war and peace can blur into near-irrelevance, and 'victory' just means today was a good day, with no guarantees for what may happen tomorrow. Instead, we will live in a world of permanent low-level conflict, often unnoticed, undeclared and unending, and one in which even our allies may also be our competitors. We are already in a time when, especially in the context of the current confrontation between Russia and the West, there is talk of the 'weaponisation' of this and that, from information to – bizarrely – football hooliganism. Yes, really: when Russian *fanaty* clashed with rival British fans in France for the Euro 2016 tournament, a 'Whitehall source' told the *Observer* newspaper, with more righteousness than plausibility, that 'it looks like a continuation of the hybrid warfare deployed by Putin'.

When everything can be weaponised, does this not then become meaningless? To an extent, that is a fair point, but even if all things are weaponisable, some are more weaponisable than others. This book is a field guide to the new way of war, or maybe *a* new way of war, or even the new world of war. It is not so much a prediction as an introduction to a potential future trajectory – as we have been reminded by COVID-19, life takes all kinds of unexpected turns, some of which can change the world. It would be easy to see the future described here as dystopian, one of eternal conflict, in which everything from charity to the law can be mobilised as a weapon. Yet I would certainly rather be targeted by disconcerting memes than nuclear missiles, and there are, fortunately, no artillery barrages in information war. This is by no means a vision of a future of bloodless conflicts – people die from economic sanctions, anti-vaccine disinformation and health budget corruption too, after all – but of at least a less bloody one, in which direct state-to-state war is increasingly priced out of the mainstream. It is also a world where the good guys, if they get their acts together, can use the same instruments as effectively as the baddies. Yes, I use those terms tongue-in-cheek – in geopolitics everyone is self-interested, rarely wholly good or bad, but variously ugly – yet nonetheless one can draw faint and fuzzy lines between those powers more or less committed to stability and a rules-based international order, and those generally willing to challenge both.

Ultimately, though, this is not a piece of advocacy. Like it or not, this is one way the world may be turning: it simply behoves us to be thinking about it now. It is all very well to complain about how other, smarter, more agile and ruthless powers may be using these instruments against us, but if all we do is react, we will always be complaining. Nothing, after all, is more powerful when weaponised than intellect and imagination.

London, April 2021

CHAPTER 1

The Renaissance of
Weaponisation

*It is early on the morning of 23 February 2014 at Vladimir
Putin's Novo-Ogaryovo residence, west of Moscow. An all-
night meeting to discuss the crisis in neighbouring Ukraine,
where popular protests have brought down Moscow-friendly
president Viktor Yanukovych, is just breaking up. Putin turns to
his security chief and tells him that 'we must start working on
returning Crimea to Russia'. Russian until 1954, and still the
home of Moscow's Black Sea Fleet, Ukraine's Crimean Peninsula
is as much of sentimental as strategic value.*

*Protests in Crimea supporting the new, pro-European Ukrainian
government are soon met with rival demonstrations. Along
with genuine enthusiasts for returning to Moscow's control are
Cossacks, members of the notorious Night Wolves motorcycle
gang (with whom Putin had ridden) and thuggish 'local self-
defence volunteers'. Many of these turn out to be members of
the two main Crimean organised crime groups, Salem and
Basmaki. It took a carefully judged mix of threats and promises*

from agents of Russia's Federal Security Service to get these blood-enemies working together, but, for the moment, they are. An orchestrated campaign of rallies magnifies and radicalises genuine resentment about a distant Ukrainian government that has neglected Crimea for years. Tame commentators warn that Crimeans face oppression from Kyiv, and agents provocateurs stir the crowd to anger.

On 27 February, Russian special forces seize local government buildings. These 'little green men' wear no insignia, and Moscow denies it has anything to do with them. The ruse is pretty transparent, but it gives Kyiv and the West some pause. Might they be mercenaries? Could this be a maverick operation by the Black Sea Fleet? This hesitation is enough for the invaders to establish commanding positions, bottling up Ukrainian garrisons and sealing the neck of the peninsula. Meanwhile, Moscow has been offering commanders within the peninsula's Ukrainian forces promotions and glory if they switch sides. The GRU, Russian military intelligence, deploys a mix of agents, disinformation and cyberattacks to break communications links with Kyiv. The actions of these undisciplined 'volunteers' are of little tactical value, despite the mysteriously new weapons they tote, but they help provide a screen of deniability, as Russia's forces methodically lock down the peninsula.

By 1 March, they have imposed their own Crimean prime minister – linked to those 'volunteers' – and forced those defenders not defecting to surrender. Russian reinforcements openly sail and fly in to secure the region. Scarcely a shot has been fired (only five people died: two civilians, two Ukrainian soldiers and one 'volunteer' who may have fumbled his own gun), but Crimea has been taken, in an operation in which subversion, criminality and misdirection matter at least as much as military force.

To some, this operation was something new, the first true 'hybrid war' conquest. Although deception and treachery were hardly novel, nonetheless a whole industry of pundits, analysts and writers dedicated to uncovering a supposed 'new way of war' was born. Is this just the most muscular end of the spectrum of diplomacy and statecraft, or something different in the nature of conflict, or simply business as usual? Maybe our vocabulary itself is not up to the task.

WHAT'S IN A NAME?

Hybrid War. Grey Zone Warfare. Asymmetric War. Tolerance Warfare. Unrestricted War. Non-Linear Warfare. A plethora of equally unhelpful new terms has emerged. Indeed, to some it is the 'Gerasimov Doctrine', a fiendish brainchild of the Russian Chief of the General Staff, General Valery Gerasimov. There is no such doctrine. I should know, as I incautiously and light-heartedly made it up as the title of an article, never believing it would be taken as gospel. The moral of the story is beware snappy titles, as they may end up having more impact than everything you write under them. But if the 'Gerasimov Doctrine' had not emerged, probably something else would have caught the commentariat's fancy. After all, everyone seems to want or need to believe that something new is emerging. In Helsinki, there is now even a European Centre of Excellence for Countering Hybrid Threats, even if there is no real consensus about what these threats may be. For that matter, Moscow is equally determined to believe that NATO has its own way of *gibridnaya voina* – hybrid war – whose mystical arts allow it to foment rebellions against Russian allies in the Arab world and post-Soviet Eurasia.

The main theme is one of mixed methods. The Chinese notion of Unrestricted Warfare, developed in the 1990s, argues that against a technologically more advanced and militarily more powerful enemy, one can still win, by shifting the conflict into economics, terrorism, even the law. In the West, the Centre of Excellence defines a 'hybrid threat' as 'an action conducted by state or non-state actors, whose goal is to undermine or harm a target by combining overt and covert military and non-military means'. Hybrid war – a term originally coined by the American military thinker Frank Hoffman specially to understand how a non-state force such as the Hezbollah militant movement in Lebanon could take on a conventional military like Israel's – has assumed an even broader meaning, to denote the combining of battlefield combat, covert subversion, disinformation, cyberattacks and anything else one side or the other can throw into the mix.

With this came the 'weaponisation wave', as the notion of items and concepts not usually connected with conflict – slander, weather, cute cat pictures – suddenly became part of mainstream media and thus political discourse. (Cute cats? The idea is that toxic messages combined with appealing and shareable social media posts circulate more widely.) The term – used in this book's title half seriously, half in self-mockery – has exploded into public use. Sociologist Greggor Mattson has found that while the term 'weaponisation' has been around for decades, it really took off in general use in 2017 – presumably not unconnected with the 2016 US presidential elections and claims of Russian interference – such that it not only seemed to erode the boundaries between civilian life and uncivil conflict but also reflected a kind of nostalgic amnesia for a lost world that had never really existed, where these two were kept rigidly apart.

Suddenly, everything can be weaponised as part of the expanding array (arsenal, even) of military metaphors all around us. The irony is that just as the language of real war is becoming blandly euphemistic (with 'delivery systems' causing 'collateral damage'), civilian speech becomes more martial. Beyond the 'War on Drugs' and the 'Battle Against COVID' (British prime minister Boris Johnson even hailed news of vaccines as proof that the 'scientific cavalry' were 'coming over the brow of the hill'), everything now seems couched in military terminology. In part this may reflect the new age in which a terrorist's bomb or a rival's sanctions could hit anyone, any time, leaving us feeling like reluctant conscripts on an invisible battlefield.

But this whole notion of some substantively 'new way of war' is problematic. Yes, the unprecedented interconnectivity of the modern world creates opportunities for states to fight without fighting. Yes, as will be discussed in the next chapter, outright state-to-state warfare of the old stabbing-and-shooting kind has become less useful and less affordable. But every war since one gang of cavemen squared off against another over possession of the driest cave has been 'hybrid'. Only in video games do you win a war by killing every one of the enemy. Instead, wars are an extreme form of coercive diplomacy, intrinsically political acts, ways of imposing your will on another by degrading their ability to resist. Skewering their soldiers and levelling their cities is just a means to an end and is only likely to work when combined with efforts to undermine their fighting spirit.

This is what British soldier-turned-theorist Basil Liddell Hart meant when he wrote that in 'all decisive campaigns, the dislocation of the enemy's psychological and physical balance has been the vital prelude to his overthrow'. Or what veteran American scholar-diplomat George Kennan called political warfare, 'the employment of all the means at a nation's command, short of war, to achieve its national objectives. Such operations are both overt and covert. They range from such overt actions as political alliances, economic measures . . . and "white" propaganda to such covert operations as clandestine support of "friendly" foreign elements, "black" psychological warfare and even encouragement of underground resistance in hostile states.' Liddell Hart was writing in 1954, though, and Kennan in 1948.

Indeed, these days, everyone's officer cadets have to read Sun Tzu, the Chinese philosopher-general who, 2,500 years ago, penned such aphorisms as 'all warfare is based on deception' and 'the supreme art of war is to subdue the enemy without fighting'. He was not so much saying anything new as codifying what every general before and since should know. Viking chieftains would unleash their berserkers, frothing with battle-fury and clad in bearskins, not just as shock troops but to terrify the enemy. Fourteenth-century Mongol armies sent out raiding parties dragging branches behind their horses to whip up clouds of dust to look like the main advance. The defection in 1435 of the Duke of Burgundy, carefully cultivated by France's Charles VII, marked a turning point in the Hundred Years' War with England. And so on: demoralise, misdirect, subvert. Today's world may offer new ways of messing with the enemy's mind and morale, but the essence remains the same.

BEYOND NEO-MEDIEVALISM

When the state's intelligence network received news that their old enemies planned to seize one of their outlying possessions, a series of operations was launched in response. First of all, influential figures in the enemy capital were encouraged to suggest that this attack was an irrelevant sideshow not worth pursuing, and they were handsomely paid for their lobbying. Secondly, eight sealed containers of poison were secretly transported to the region in question, with the aim of contaminating the attacking force's water supply, and making it look like illness, not covert action. Indeed, businesspeople who traded with the enemy were encouraged to suggest that the attackers foolishly drank from waters known to be bad, to amplify the deception.

This operation actually took place in 1570 under the supervision of the Council of Ten, the Venetian Republic's formidable intelligence overseers. Through a Papal envoy, who had been recruited as a Venetian agent, they learned that the Ottoman Turks planned to seize Spalato, one of their colonies in Dalmatia. Direct military action was not possible, as Venice was having to conserve its forces for a defence of Cyprus, on which Ottoman Sultan Selim II clearly had designs. Hence, a combination of intrigue in Istanbul, disinformation spread by Croatian fishermen who sold their catch in Ottoman-held ports, and outright terrorism, all to do what mere force of arms might not. And it worked: Spalato – today known as Split – remained Venetian until 1797.

Back in the 1970s, the scholar Hedley Bull raised the notion that the future may be found in the past, that we face not a single (utopian or dystopian) world government, but instead a 'neo-medievalism', where the sovereignty of regions, countries and supra-national bodies are partial and overlapping. In medieval times, a European feudal ruler would at once have to share authority with his vassals below him, as well as the Pope or the Holy Roman Emperor above. To Bull, this would be a fine thing, with individual rights and overarching senses of the common good replacing or moderating the selfishness of sovereign states. Maybe.

The 1648 Peace of Westphalia ended the Thirty Years' War, a miserably brutal religious struggle that devastated Germany and marked the start of the era of true national sovereignty. States were assumed to have absolute authority within their own borders – and none beyond them. In the twentieth century, emerging notions of international law began to dilute this, along with the rise of transnational corporations and grand ideological blocs. The collapse of the Soviet Union at the end of 1991 lifted the threat of nuclear Armageddon, at least for a while, but the new world that is emerging is one in which the power of the state is both great and brittle. Money, people, goods, information and ideas all flow around the world more quickly than ever, and every time they cross national borders, they weaken them, just a little.

In the future, we may well look back on the Westphalian era as the aberration, but rather than a new medieval era – when wars were as common as they were ugly – perhaps a better model is the Italian Renaissance, a time when city-states and principalities competed and cooperated with equal ease. The age of inter-state shooting wars is not over, of course, but they have become mercifully rarer. So, is the world at peace, are nations happily coexisting in the name of the common good? Hardly. Rather, our present notions of war, as something formally declared and ended, fought largely on the battlefield, where laws are meant to protect non-combatants and define the acceptable forms of force, are becoming less and less relevant. Instead, war is outsourced and sublimated, fought as often through culture and credit, faith and famine, as direct force of arms.

The Renaissance of Weaponisation

The fourteenth- to sixteenth-century Renaissance was an era not just of mercenary companies and short, sharp military confrontations, it was also one in which today's enemy was tomorrow's ally (and vice versa), and where banking, culture and information were weapons as effective as the sword and pike. Street-corner gossip was mobilised as political ammunition and 'fake news' increasingly embedded in art and diplomacy by a new, mobile and transnational class of mercenary diplomats, emissaries, opinion-formers and spies.

RENAISSANCE OF THE RENAISSANCE

Costantini de' Servi was a renowned artist and sculptor, famed as a garden designer and welcome at courts from Persia's to England's, even though in hindsight he rarely seemed actually to complete any gardens. Yet he certainly contrived to be on hand whenever some major geopolitical event was in the making. He was a spy working for the Medici of Florence, and a peddler of lies and doctored information. In 1611, Florence was trying to arrange a political marriage between Caterina Medici and Henry, Prince of Wales. When the teenage prince balked at not having met his proposed bride, the Florentine ambassador floundered. But de' Servi presented a sketch of a beautiful young woman, claiming – wholly without foundation – that it was Caterina. Had Henry not died shortly thereafter from typhoid, the result of this timely deployment of 'fake news' could well have been a dynastic marriage that would have changed the European balance of power of the age.

Power is about perception, influence about imagination. When Renaissance princes competed to attract the finest artists and poets and sculptors to their courts, it was not simply for their own pleasure, it was also a battlefront in the political and cultural wars being waged between the city-states. Such patronage demonstrated wealth and a city's or a lineage's cultural authority. The Cattedrale di Santa Maria del Fiore in Florence, St Peter's Basilica in Rome and the Sforza Castle in Milan were soaring statements of power and ambition encoded in brick and marble and gold. Likewise, China's first solo mission to Mars, Tianwen-1, and the US's Artemis programme to land a man and a woman on the Moon's south pole by 2024 are about projecting leadership, technological power and ambition as much as exploration and science.

Building cathedrals and commissioning statues were also boasts of resources, whether financial or political. After all, the one could become the other. When the Vatican taxed Christians across Europe to have Michelangelo paint the roof of the Sistine Chapel, this was not just about funding art. It was also about power, generating resources that could be diverted to other projects and enrich grandees along the way, buying their loyalty with a gesture of apparent piety. Power begets money, and money begets power.

Today we are obsessed with the dangers of 'fake news' and disinformation, and likewise the Renaissance saw the rise of information warfare, whether to shore up a city-state's legitimating narrative or undermine a rival's. This was a time when politics and literature, scholarship and propaganda went hand in hand and cities fought with pen as much as sword, over a period of years. Florentine humanist Coluccio Salutati duelled Milanese chancellor Antonio Loschi through rival texts such the latter's *Invective Against Florentines*, and Gian Galeazzo Visconti, Duke of Milan, admitted that 'a thousand Florentine cavalry do me less damage than Salutati's letters and speeches'. This was a struggle built on the earlier literary clashes between Leonardo Bruni's *Laudatio of Florence* and Pier Candido Decembrio's response, his *Panegyricus of Milan*. The aim was to demonstrate the cultural and historical authority of their respective cities and uphold or undermine Visconti's claims to dominance over Italy. Today's practices of national branding, the outsourcing of soft power and the covert and overt purchase of good news coverage and social media likes all have their parallels in these narrative struggles.

In the Renaissance, civil unrest, rebellions by subject cities, and rural insurrections were a daily reality. These were gleefully weaponised for factional and inter-state gain. Francesco Bertazuolo's gang terrified and destabilised Venice's Terraferma inland territories, for example, growing to a size of several hundred bandits, while he himself lived openly in the town of Salò, in a house whose owner he had murdered. A full-time brigand, Bertazuolo was also a part-time Milanese asset, periodically stirring up trouble for Venice to order. Likewise, the Papacy supported the Pazzi family when they tried to kill Lorenzo de' Medici in 1478 and install a new regime in Florence, just as it had backed equally unsuccessful rebels against King Ferdinand of Naples. Terrorism and insurgency were then, as now, instruments of statecraft.

LASCIATE OGNI SPERANZA?

On 17 July 2014, Malaysia Airlines Flight 17 (MH17) was flying across eastern Ukraine, taking 283 passengers from Amsterdam to Kuala Lumpur. Suddenly, a missile launched by a Russian-made Buk (Beech) M-1 launcher blasted it with shrapnel, bringing it down near the village of Hrabove, killing everyone on board. Moscow had provided the weapon to its proxy forces fighting against Kyiv, but not the training and radar systems that would have allowed them to tell a passenger aircraft from a Ukrainian warplane. The rebels briefly crowed about their success in shooting down what they thought was a government military aircraft, before they realised what they had done. Moscow swung into action, launching a massive propaganda campaign to muddy the waters and claim MH17 had been downed by anything but a Russian missile, while seeking to hide any evidence of its role.

The force that would do most to expose the truth of what happened was not a government or media conglomerate but a newly formed investigative citizen journalism outfit called Bellingcat, which had until recently been run out of its founder's flat. Volunteers scoured Russian social media for posts identifying those involved. Locals who had seen the Buk launchers trundle their way from Russia – and then hurriedly withdraw – uploaded photos taken with their smartphones, pictures which could then be geolocated, their positions confirmed by studying the surrounding topography. Online and in the regular media, Bellingcat's amateurs and enthusiasts could take on a powerful, cynical state in narrative warfare – and win.

It is tempting to be a doomsayer, to note the way that the new Renaissance is a time of uncertainty and instability, in which we seem to be hurtling towards anarchy at an ever-faster rate. *Lasciate ogni speranza* – abandon all hope – reads the gateway to hell in Dante's epic poem *Inferno*, but then again Dante is also considered the father of the Italian language and an example of the creative dynamism in fields from arts and architecture to banking and statecraft that took place in the Renaissance.

The Renaissance of Weaponisation

Much of the research and writing to date about emerging forms of conflict looks at one or more specific sources of threat, such as disinformation, hacking or 'lawfare'. Much of it is also apocalyptic, focusing exclusively on the problems. This book seeks not only to look more comprehensively at the new world of non-kinetic conflict or no-holds-barred statecraft, at signs of a growing redefinition of the global order, but also to offer some practical and often counterintuitive examples of how we can not only protect ourselves from these challenges but take advantage of them.

One could argue that it is irrelevant whether one dies on the battlefield or in a refugee camp, whether one loses one's job to economic warfare or a bombing raid. Either way, there is a toll of the dead and destitute. Yet in the main, these new forms of national competition are less lethal, and that should surely be considered a step forward. They may often be harder to deter, but deterrence, the mainstay of Cold War security thinking, is at best a stopgap. Deterrence doesn't make friends; it just prevents overt conflict. It may actually reinforce assumptions of hostility. What is known in International Relations jargon as the 'Security Dilemma' explains how states with only defensive intent may still find themselves at war, not least as, if I seek to deter you, I admit that I see you as a threat. It certainly pushes the conflict into new arenas.

Furthermore, conflict is being democratised. Only states can build nuclear missiles or field mechanised divisions, but individuals, corporations and communities can engage in narrative warfare, or take out a legal case, or boycott a product. Ultimately, these methods can be used for positive goals, not just zero-sum national interest. In many ways, Bellingcat and all sorts of ventures like it, for example, reflect the bright mirror-image to the gloomy world of perpetual conflict.

This book is not necessarily intended to be read as a prediction. Perhaps it is best thought of as a cautionary tale, whether as to how especially unscrupulous states will turn the elemental forms of the modern world against us, or how we may all be sucked into zero-sum non-military conflicts over resources, opportunity and status. Or a how-to field guide to the coming age? Either way, it is a quick and opinionated overview of a monstrously complex set of processes and challenges and must, as a result, take short cuts and make over-simplifications. It is not, however, meant to be an entirely hopeless saga. Dante made his way through Hell and, after more than 14,000 lines of verse, reached Paradise. I cannot promise quite such a journey, but there is certainly no need to abandon all hope.

WANT TO KNOW MORE?

Useful books on the emerging (and continuing) forms of conflict in the modern world are many, but a few worth noting (not that I agree with them all) include Linda Robinson et al., *Modern Political Warfare* (RAND, 2018); Sean McFate, *Goliath: Why the West Isn't Winning. And What We Must Do About It* (Michael Joseph, 2019); Thomas Rid, *Active Measures: The Secret History of Disinformation and Political Warfare* (Macmillan, 2020); and David Kilcullen, *The Dragons and the Snakes: How the Rest Learned to Fight the West* (Hurst, 2020). A collection of essays for the European Council on Foreign Relations edited by Mark Leonard, *Connectivity Wars* (2016), is also very useful. As to the classics, though, there are numerous translations of Sun Tzu's *The Art of War*, even a graphic novel adaptation, but Norman Angell's *The Great Illusion* (Putnam, 1911), while rather longer and less packed with nifty aphorisms, also in its own way questions the fundamentals of national power.

On the sorry tale of the 'Gerasimov Doctrine', you can read my article of the same name in the *Berlin Policy Journal*, 28 April 2020 (https://berlinpolicyjournal.com/the-gerasimov-doctrine/), and Greggor Mattson's study of the 'weaponisation wave' can be found in his article 'Weaponization: Ubiquity and Metaphorical Meaningfulness' in the journal *Metaphor & Symbol*, volume 35, issue 4 (2020). Speaking of the use of language as aggression, Qiao Liang and Wang Xianshui's *Unrestricted Warfare* (Albatross, 2020) has been published in English with the addition of the inaccurate and tendentious subtitle, *China's Master Plan to Destroy America*.

PART I

Ain't Gonna Study (Shooting) War No More

CHAPTER 2

The Deweaponisation of Warfare?

In the fourteenth century, the Florentine Republic had more than its fair share of disputes with the Papacy. Florence was concerned about the expansion of the Papal States that the Vatican was creating across Central Italy and, fearing Pope Gregory XI would turn against them in 1375 after the conclusion of his war against Milan, they deployed a characteristic asymmetric mix of statecraft and finance. A massive sum of 130,000 florins was paid to the most respected of the Pope's mercenary commanders, the Englishman John Hawkwood, in return for a guarantee that he would not march against Florence. And where did they get this fortune? By taxing the religious institutions within their domain, to deliver a double blow against the Church.

Nonetheless, war was inevitable. Florence concluded an alliance with Milan and then sent agents to stir up revolts within the Papal States. Gregory responded by excommunicating Florence's leaders from the community of the Church and imposing economic sanctions on the city's merchants. His mercenary armies suppressed the risings in the Papal States, often with brutal abandon, and in 1377 seized the city of Bologna, until then a Florentine ally. Eventually, hostilities ended in 1378. Although the original demand had been that Florence pay a full million florins as restitution, this was haggled down to 200,000. In return, Florence received a series of guarantees and the lifting of the religious sanctions placed upon it.

This was a relatively unremarkable war by the standards of the Renaissance, but one of the most interesting aspects of it was the name it acquired: the War of the Eight Saints. These were not actual saints – far from it – but rather the eight officials of an emergency committee established by the Florentine government to oversee the taxation of Church assets. This would prove crucial in allowing the republic to bear the costs of the war, estimated at some 2.5 million florins.

The irony is that the reason this could be done is because states at the time raised money in frequently shambolic ways, often relying on forced loans and one-off levies rather than regular taxation. As a result, public finances routinely tapped only a small share of the national wealth, which was a problem – but at least it also left ample room for such ad hoc measures as the Eight Saints. Modern states, of course, have turned taxation into an art, and public finances generally account for around a third of total national wealth. That pays for our pensions and healthcare, armies and spies, but leaves us with fewer options, short of the kind of deficit financing with which we have handled the COVID-19 crisis, when we want to pay for wars.

THE PRICE OF WAR

Are we pricing good old-fashioned war out of existence? It would be nice to think so. We certainly spend more on preparing for war than ever before. A Second World War Spitfire fighter plane cost around £12,500, which would be equivalent to about £822,000 today. On the other hand, the new F-35 Lightning IIs Britain is now buying cost £92 million each. To put it another way, you could get 112 Spitfires for a single F-35, or buy all 640 fighters the RAF deployed during the Battle of Britain for, even in today's money, less than 6 F-35s. The tools of modern war are very expensive indeed.

At least there one can point to capabilities different by whole orders of magnitude: an F-35 (if it works as promised, that is, but that's a whole other story) can engage multiple targets at once, even over the horizon, while flying at more than three times the speed of a Spitfire. But GI Joe in 1941 cost $160 to kit out fully, from his khaki uniform to his bolt-action M1 rifle. His modern counterpart costs about $18,000 to equip in all his camouflaged and high-tech glory, or almost 6 times as much when adjusted for inflation. Yet while his M4 carbine can fire more rounds, more quickly, to a longer range and often with greater accuracy, and he has body armour, night-vision goggles and a radio, he can still freeze in panic, can still only be in one place at a time, and only has one life, alas. Besides which, all those high-tech gadgets require batteries that are often heavy and prone to run down at the most inconvenient moment.

The cost of war extends to each individual munition. The most up-to-date version of the US Patriot long-range ground-to-air missile costs up to $5 million per round (that's just the missile, not including the associated launch vehicle, radars and the like). This sounds like a bargain if it shoots down the nuclear missile that was going to wipe out your capital city, or a $215 million Russian Tu-160M bomber. That's not always how modern war works, though. In 2017, General David Perkins, commander of the United States Army Training and Doctrine Command, revealed that a 'very close ally' – generally assumed to be Israel or Saudi Arabia – used a Patriot to shoot down a small, off-the-shelf commercial quadcopter drone that would have cost $200–300 if bought from Amazon. As he drily observed, 'on the economic exchange-ratio, I'm not sure that's good'.

After all, modern wars are voracious and discriminating in their appetites. It is an often-quoted truism that 'amateurs talk about tactics, but professionals study logistics'. A modern tank gets maybe a little more than 0.5 miles to the gallon, for example. Indeed, the US military is the world's single largest consumer of fuel. In the Second World War, it used on average a gallon per soldier per day, but that has now climbed to fully 16 gallons, especially because of the increasing use of thirsty aircraft to ferry soldiers around, support them on the battlefield and, yes, supply all the necessities of war. More rapid-fire guns means more bullets to haul around; smarter weapons are also pricier ones.

According to the Cost of War programme at Brown University's Watson Institute, in the first 20 years of the twenty-first century, the US's 'War on Terror' – including invading Afghanistan and Iraq – cost the country $6.4 trillion through direct and indirect costs. By contrast, the decade-long Vietnam War cost an estimated $168 billion, or $1 trillion in today's money. As for the 12 years of the Napoleonic Wars, they cost Britain £831 million in the coin of the day, or £75 billion ($93 billion) in modern terms. Wars aren't what they used to be; they are rather more expensive.

COSTS OF DIFFERENT KINDS

But it's not just about dollars, pounds or even roubles: other costs of war have also escalated rapidly. First of all, however much inhumanity there still seems to be in the world, there also appears to have emerged a growing unwillingness to spend lives willy-nilly. Once, generals could accept the deaths of thousands in a single day's carnage with, if not equanimity, a conviction that this was what war meant. (While, as Lord Wellington is meant to have said when one of his artillerymen had sight of Napoleon at Waterloo, 'it is not the business of commanders to be firing upon one another'.) Now, things are different.

In 1983, a truck bomb driven by two members of the group Islamic Jihad exploded at the barracks of a US Marine detachment in Beirut as part of a multinational peacekeeping force: 241 were killed, and 13 more later died of their wounds. There were retaliatory strikes, but for all the bluster from Washington, it was soon clear that the political mood had shifted. Within four months, the Americans were leaving Lebanon. Ten years later, and the deaths of eighteen US servicemen in the 1993 Battle of Mogadishu – immortalised in the film *Black Hawk Down* (2001) – not only changed US policy in Somalia, it also left Washington gun-shy of future potential deployments, most notably in response to the Rwandan genocide the next year.

Of course, democracies are most subject to the wave of public revulsion that can often follow the sombre images of flag-draped coffins and sobbing widows (and, now, widowers). Yet even rather more authoritarian states can find themselves nervously aware of the political costs of treating their soldiers like so much ammunition, to be expended as the needs of battle dictate. This may once have been how the Soviet Union fought, but by the time of its ill-judged intervention in Afghanistan, 1979–89, it was already having to respond, first with censorship (initially it was claimed quite simply that there was no war, until the flow of returning soldiers made that less and less tenable), then with attempts to set up proper medical evacuation and treatment services. Post-Soviet Russia, awkwardly balanced between democracy and dictatorship, had to be even more careful. Public outcry about military and civilian casualties helped force Moscow, in effect, to call a draw during its first war to quell the rebellious Chechens in 1994–96. Then, the Kremlin combined censorship, a reliance on long-range firepower and the recruitment of its own Chechen fighters during the successful rematch of 1999–2009. It was precisely concerns about a backlash at the thought of young Ivan coming home in a zinc box while in pursuit of imperial adventures, about which the public cared little, that drove Vladimir Putin later to use local auxiliaries, thugs and adventurers in his undeclared war in southeastern Ukraine from 2014 and mercenaries in Syria from 2015 and Libya from 2018.

This also reflects the dramatic change in the speed, access and coverage of media. In an age when anyone with a Twitter feed or an Instagram account can be considered a media outlet, by definition everything becomes public; the only question is how quickly and with what spin. The days when wars could be curated, when a handful of journalists and chroniclers, newspaper proprietors and TV anchors could establish the narrative, are long gone. In ancient times, this was rather easier. King Esarhaddon's reign over Assyria in the seventh century BC was marked by a crushing military defeat at the hands of the rival Elamites and then another in Egypt. The solution adopted by the unknown figure compiling the Chronicle of Esarhaddon? Simple, just omit these setbacks altogether. Other monarchs might be more entrepreneurial in their management of the narrative. When Prince Dmitry Donskoi of Moscow defeated the Mongol-Tatar army at Kulikovo in 1380, he had his tame chroniclers ready to portray it as a decisive victory freeing Russia of foreign domination. That a Mongol army returned to sack and burn Moscow two years later, and that the Russian princes still had to pay tribute to them for another century, was conveniently downplayed in the story.

In 1782, Benjamin Franklin created a newspaper featuring a gory tale of a dastardly English plot to pay Native Americans for colonials' scalps. He distributed the newspaper to his friends, and they forwarded it on to theirs, and before long, the gruesome story had made it into other papers. The minor detail was that this was all 'fake news', but who could confirm the real facts of the matter, or even wanted to? Franklin had successfully stirred up anger against the English king – but also painted the Native Americans as a barbarian fifth column, sentiments that would be revived during the inconclusive War of 1812 and contributed to the harsh treatment they would receive at its end.

Arguably, it was only in the 1850s, when *The Times* of London sent William Howard Russell to cover the Crimean War – which he did with a merciless eye for the terrible conditions facing the ordinary soldiers and the bumbling of the War Office – that the modern concept of the war correspondent emerged, and it became a topic of immediate currency, not the preserve of the historian and the pamphleteer. By the time of the First World War, this had led to a new climate of censorship and the beginning of the notion of the accredited – and, the authorities hoped, thus house-trained – correspondent. Already, though, as the telegraph and the telephone made communication instantaneous, the newsreel, a short film magazine of news and documentary features, was increasingly a staple at the cinemas. The struggle between the managers, manipulators and miners of information was becoming ever more tense.

Today, while states have arguably never been as systematic and as eager to try and control the narratives around their wars, it is becoming increasingly hard for any but the most totalitarian to do so. The Vietnam War was arguably the first in which the state found itself conclusively unable to master the media, and the – frankly, sensationalist – coverage in the US of the North Vietnamese 1968 Tet Offensive epitomised this. It was a serious military defeat for the North but, perhaps in reaction to gung-ho earlier reporting, it generated a wave of critical coverage in the US media that presented it actually as a Northern achievement. This pushed the White House towards reassessing its commitment to the war. Television, a medium with which the government had not yet come to terms, and which could bring not so much the war, but its own perspective of the war into every American's living room, played a key role in this.

That was before social media, though. Moscow's attempts to claim non-involvement in Ukraine's Donbas have been undermined in part by the propensity of its own soldiers to post cheery selfies in front of street signs or other geolocatable landmarks on Vkontakte, Russia's Facebook equivalent. So too, Damascus's traditional media blackout on some of the more vicious aspects of its attempts to reimpose its rule have been undermined by a new generation of citizen journalists streaming the news and their own experiences around the world. As will be discussed later, hashtags, memes and selfies have become weapons of new narrative wars in their own right, and have proliferated as much as the ubiquitous AK-47 rifle.

Everything leaks. Thanks to whistle-blowers and online activists, hackers and careless social media addicts, information has burst through and over the dams and dykes states once could rely on to channel and block its flow. Combined with the new willingness of society critically to assess the human and economic costs of war, and indeed the massive increase in the expense of fighting full-scale industrial and then post-industrial conflict, what once seemed the hobby of military aristocrats and inbred monarchs has now become very much a last resort of policymakers around the world.

ALL WARS END UP BEING JUST WARS

Then there is the apparently increasing influence of international law and the court of global opinion, and to understand this, we need to look at its evolution. So long as there has been organised warfare, there have been attempts to regulate its right and proper conduct, from when it was just, to how it ought to be waged. The Indian epic the *Mahābhārata*, written, edited and serially redrafted, likely over a period of six centuries from the third century BC, is as much a philosophical tract as a legendary cycle. Within its 200,000 lines are debates about the essence of *dharmayuddha*, 'just war'. The conclusion is that wars should be fought only when attempts to resolve them have failed, and not from anger of the moment. They should be waged with such proportionality and humanity as possible, sparing the helpless and eschewing unduly vicious means, such as poisoned arrows.

The heart of such early notions was morality rather than regulation, though. The Greek philosopher Aristotle felt that war was moral if waged to avoid becoming enslaved – but also to enslave those who were 'natural slaves'. In other words, those who deserved it, largely by foolishly not being Greek. The Roman notion of *ius gentium*, the 'law of nations', was likewise essentially normative, a notion of international law based on values and a shared understanding of what was right and wrong. Later, the early Christian theologian Augustine of Hippo tried to square the circle of a theoretical commitment to pacifism with the realities of a world full of warlords and would-be conquerors. In his *The City of God* (c.413–26), he asserted that to sit back and let the sinful triumph was itself a sin, coining the phrase 'just war' for purely defensive conflicts, wars fought in the name of peace. The 'wise man will wage Just Wars' and not lament their necessity, 'for if they were not just, he would not wage them'. QED.

This was all about the morality of war, and as such often delightfully subjective for those who would drape a flimsy cloak of justice around their martial pursuits. In 1095, Pope Urban II warned Christendom that 'an accursed race, a race utterly alienated from God' had taken Jerusalem and the Holy Lands and incited the First Crusade. This began what would be almost two hundred years of vicious conflict, full of massacre, treachery and persecution on both sides. But these were just wars: successive popes said so.

In 1452, another pope, Nicholas V, issued *Dum Diversas* ('Until Different'), a papal bull endorsing the enslavement of 'Saracens, pagans and any other unbelievers'. In 1513, this was used by Spain to claim a God-given right to seize the lands of the New World, waging bloody and terrible wars of conquest to subdue the Aztecs, Inca, Maya and other nations of South America. But these were just wars: popes and monarchs agreed.

When, under Genghis Khan, the Mongols swept forth in the campaigns that would win them an empire stretching from northern China to Central Europe, they did so firm in the knowledge that Blue Sky Tengri, greatest of their shamanic spirit-deities, had granted them a mandate to conquer all the lands under the heavens. These were just wars: the spirits had decreed.

The Confederates fought in the American Civil War in the name of 'states' rights', just as the 1846–48 Mexican–American War was driven and rationalised on the basis of the US's 'manifest destiny'. On a very different scale, Nazis embarked on their wars of conquest claiming a right to *Lebensraum*, 'living space', and to defend the purity of the Aryan race. Every war can be framed as a just one, if left to the warriors.

LAWS, WARS AND THE RISE OF THE BORELORDS

The first notion of outright laws defining the parameters and conduct of conflict were agreements between states: treaties ending wars, defining boundaries and establishing tribute. Around 2100 BC, the Mesopotamian city-states of Umma and Lagash agreed their mutual border and carved the consequent agreement on a stone pillar the height of a man. Over a thousand years later, Ramses II of Egypt and Hattusili III, king of the Hittites, agreed 'eternal peace and brotherhood' between their nations. They inscribed it on a silver tablet, witnessed by 'the mountains and rivers of the lands of Egypt; the sky; the earth; the great sea; the winds; the clouds' such that whomever broke the treaty would face the wrath of the gods who 'shall destroy his house, his land and his servants'.

Maybe it was the gods that made all the difference. Certainly such grandiosely named agreements as the Perpetual Peace signed between Byzantium and the Sassanids in 532, the 1502 Treaty of Perpetual Peace between Scotland and England, the 1686 Treaty of Eternal Peace between Poland and Russia or the 1940 Treaty of Eternal Friendship between Hungary and Yugoslavia all proved of greater or lesser volatility. (The last of those was broken within six months.)

Ain't Gonna Study (Shooting) War No More

Only much later did it become possible to think and talk of the notion of international law as something beyond and above the treaties of the day. In the words of one former British military officer with experience in both Iraq and Afghanistan, 'the age of the warlords has been replaced by the age of the boring international lawyer, the grey diplomat. It should sit uncomfortably with me as a career soldier, but anyone who has had to explain to angry parents why they won't see their boy again should welcome it.'

But the rise of these, let's call them 'borelords', has been a slow and halting process, since the beginning of the seventeenth century, when Dutch jurist and diplomat Hugo Grotius published his work *On the Law of War and Peace* (1625). The 1648 Treaties of Westphalia that ended the murderous European wars of religion enshrined the notions of state sovereignty, the principle that each state, large or small, has an equal right to independence within its own borders. Even so, there was nothing like an international court to enforce it. Wars were still fought, empires built and territories won and lost, with might making right by conquest, trade war and intimidation.

After all, stronger states generally do not want to be limited and weaker ones rarely get a say. It would take the cataclysm that was the First World War, as well as the idealism of US president Woodrow Wilson, to create the League of Nations. This was a classic example of the mismatch between lofty principles and shallow self-interest, especially when the US itself ended up not joining when Senate blocked it. With defeated Germany and Bolshevik Russia not being invited, this was hardly the full premier league. That is not to say it did no good at all. Through the 1920s, it was a hub for diplomatic negotiation, but as Italian fascist leader Mussolini put it, 'the League is all very

36

well when sparrows shout, but no good at all when eagles fall out'. And the eagles would, with the rise of Fascist Italy, Nazi Germany, Stalin's USSR and an imperialist Japan, and the slide to war.

So, after the Second World War, the international community tried again. In the shadow of the Nazi concentration camps, of 75 million dead and of the atomic mushroom cloud, the United Nations was conceived, in the words of Dag Hammarskjöld, its second secretary general, 'not to lead mankind to heaven but to save humanity from hell'. It is easy to be cynical about the UN, about the well-provisioned representatives gleefully invoking diplomatic immunity to ignore New York City parking tickets, about its seemingly endless red tape and about the way members of the 'P5' – the US, Russia, China, France and the UK, the five permanent members of the Security Council – veto those resolutions that don't suit them. However, for all that, there has been a genuine, creeping revolution in international relations. It is not so much, or simply, because of the role of the UN, but rather that it represents a new recognition that in an interconnected and nuclear world, the old notion of *ius gentium*, what could almost be called international etiquette, is of common interest. The Geneva Convention on behaviour in wartime, the International Court of Justice to prosecute crimes against humanity, the 1961 Vienna Convention that enshrines the protection of diplomats, all these instruments – however they may be breached from time to time – nonetheless reflect a genuine, general understanding that there ought to be limits on state action and that the 'borelords' are part of the answer.

Besides which, the logic of Westphalian sovereignty – which in effect says that whatever a government does within its own borders is its own business – has been giving way to notions of humanitarian interventionism and 'R2P', Responsibility to Protect populations from genocide, as well as all sorts of other admirable global do-gooding. When Saddam Hussein invaded Kuwait in 1990, it triggered a US-led international response that may well have largely been motivated by a desire to stop a murderous dictator from seizing its oil reserves, but there was also a genuine sense that this was behaviour for which there was no more place in the world. Ethnic cleansing in a disintegrating Yugoslavia, genocide in Rwanda, nuclear proliferation in Iran and North Korea, Russia's annexation of Crimea: responses to such breaches of that international etiquette were of varying form and effectiveness, from military intervention, through aid and hand-wringing to economic sanctions, but what is striking is that there have been such reactions at all.

STUDY WAR NO MORE?

The point is not that the UN and international law are unable to prevent these atrocities and conflicts – but that we are surprised and outraged that they don't do a better job of it. If not laws, norms matter, and so too do global perceptions. When Moscow decided in 2014 that it needed to bring pressure to bear on Ukraine to accept that it was part of its sphere of influence, it did not simply invade; it stirred up a proxy rebellion in south-eastern Ukraine, only surging in its own troops when it looked as if government forces were going to roll over the rebels. The insurgents were vastly less effective, and often more interested in loot and macho posturing than following orders, but from the Kremlin's point of view, it was more important to maintain deniability, as much to the international community as its own sceptical population. (Unlike the Crimean annexation, the Donbas war is not at all popular at home.)

This helps explain why big, conventional, state-to-state wars are relatively rare these days. In his book *The Better Angels of Our Nature: Why Violence Has Declined* (2011), Steven Pinker makes the dramatic claim that 'today we may be living in the most peaceable era in our species' existence'. It has sparked considerable debate, often focusing on the philosophical dimensions of quite what constitutes 'peace', not least as Pinker was not just talking about war but violence of every kind. Entire books can and have been written on this topic, and one can certainly question some of his thesis, but, in very broad terms, three trends have become clear.

First of all, modern war has the potential to become very deadly, very quickly. This was evident in such conflicts as the 1980–88 Iran–Iraq War, where First World War-style trench conflicts combined with the technological terrors of modern weaponry and the medieval spectacle of human wave attacks. Iran's Operation Ramadan, 3 offensives launched across 6 weeks in 1982, saw up to 150,000 Iranians, many the scarcely trained and lightly armed *basij* militia, thrown against Iraqi mechanised divisions, which had dug in and were backed by armour. The offensive made no lasting gains – and cost perhaps 80,000 Iranian lives.

However, in part perhaps because of the scale of the potential butcher's bill, major state-versus-state conflicts have become shorter and less common since 1945. There are, of course, continually worrying potential flashpoints. The dispute over Kashmir between India and Pakistan has led to three wars and countless skirmishes and hubristic military displays since their formation in 1947 – with one more war, in 1971, fought over Bangladesh as a change of scene. Likewise, Israel has been the locus of seven or eight 'proper' wars with various of its Arab neighbours (depending on how you count them), as well as sundry counterinsurgency campaigns, military incursions and anti-terrorist missions.

Yet, as will be discussed below, there is an increasingly theatrical dimension to the Indo–Pakistani conflict, and while Israel is still engaged in a multi-theatre, multi-level struggle with Iran, the country once ostracised by its neighbours now has full diplomatic relations with Egypt and Jordan and working, if often covert, relations with Lebanon, Saudi Arabia, Iraq and even – up to a point – with Syria. Instead, wars are now typically internal, often with one or more foreign powers supporting one side or the other. They are not necessarily less bloody, though: even the casualties of the various Indo–Pakistani wars are overshadowed by the toll of inter-communal violence between Hindus, Sikhs and Muslims across former British India, which has claimed the lives of more than a million people and left 14 million more displaced.

At times, these are virtual proxy wars, such as the current struggles in Syria and Libya, at others rebellions or counterinsurgencies with outside involvement, such as in Afghanistan, Yemen and perhaps Ukraine. They are often complex, messy conflicts. In Syria, for example, this is not a straightforward struggle of the Assad government and its Russian and Iranian backers against a rebellion supported by the US and Turkey. Rather, the anti-government forces are divided across ethnic, factional and religious lines, and while Washington and Ankara did share common interests at one point, they quickly diverged. The result often looks more like a pub brawl with automatic weapons than anything more elegant.

THE THEATRE OF WAR

Even so, it is striking how important it is for states to avoid direct confrontation, even while indulging in belligerent posturing. In November 2015, a Turkish F-16 fighter shot down a Russian Sukhoi Su-24M bomber involved in operations against rebels in north-western Syria, as it briefly crossed into Turkish airspace. Moscow's initial response was furious. Vladimir Putin called it 'a stab in the back by the accomplices of terrorists', and economic sanctions saw Turkish tomatoes disappear from Russian supermarket shelves, package tours restricted and, of all things, football clubs banned from signing Turkish players. But despite fears of an escalation, Turkish president Recep Tayyip Erdoğan – an even more accomplished master of bluff and bluster than Putin – refused to back down. By 2016 the men were meeting again, and within a year, sanctions were quietly being lifted.

If anything, the Kremlin was even more circumspect when, on 7 February 2018, an assault on rebel positions in Deir ez-Zor province triggered a US response of epic proportions, involving not just rocket artillery but the whole panoply of American airpower, from huge B-52 bombers and AC-130 gunships to F-22 Raptor stealth fighters and AH-64 Apache attack helicopters. The attacking force included a sizeable contingent from the Russian Wagner mercenary company – for most of its existence essentially another arm of the Kremlin – but Moscow and the official Russian military contingent in Syria sat back and let them be pounded. According to some accounts, more than 200 Russians were killed.

This is not confined to the Russians. No one can, for example, question the bad blood between modern India and Pakistan, but even their generations-long contest over Kashmir, one

41

turbocharged by the religious enmities of Hindu and Muslim, has – mercifully – assumed something of a ritual nature of late. In February 2019, for example, a Pakistan-based terrorist group claimed responsibility for a suicide car bombing that killed forty Indian paramilitaries. With both sides frequently using terrorists as proxies, unsurprisingly India laid the blame squarely on Pakistan. Within a fortnight, Indian aircraft launched an attack over the border, claiming to have hit a terrorist training camp, and Pakistan duly retaliated. Although one Indian fighter was shot down, closer examination of both attacks demonstrated that neither side's bombs actually hit anything. Rather than supremely incompetent piloting, this actually demonstrates sophisticated crisis management. Both sides got to flex their military muscles and reassure their domestic audience, and neither risked a serious and bloody escalation.

Does that mean that we now live in an age of harmony and good neighbourliness? If only that were true. Just ask the Ukrainians, the Syrians and the Afghans, the Nigerians, the Kashmiris and the Somalis. Indeed, since the end of the Cold War, which channelled so many other rivalries and tensions into a single confrontation, one could argue that a post-ideological age is also a deeply conflicted one. Close allies compete viciously for trade deals and a technological edge, for precedence and prestige. If now we have no real enemies, the sad corollary is that we have no real friends, either.

As I write this, Azerbaijan and Armenia have just ended another short, bitter war over a disputed border region, Nagorno-Karabakh. The age of shooting wars is not totally over, of course, and this is a point to which I will return at the end of this book, but since the end of the Cold War, not only have inter-state wars remained mercifully rare, but we need to look elsewhere for the expressions of forceful competition. The end of the Manichean (if often sterile) struggle between capitalism and communism has actually unlocked so many more complex rivalries and competitions, ones that still need some kind of outlet and resolution, sublimated into all kinds of alternative realms. Perhaps more alarmingly, this is a war (of sorts) of all against all, simply differing in the intensity and form it takes. At its most extreme, the new way of war is one of constant competition, in which the forces mustered are as often deniable and non-violent, and where all states vie against each other, and do so without hope of treaty or thought of an end.

WANT TO KNOW MORE?

Beyond the books already mentioned, Hew Strachan's collection *The Changing Character of War* (OUP, 2011) is a comprehensive overview, while historian Margaret MacMillan's *War: How Conflict Shaped Us* (Profile, 2020) looks at it from the other direction, at the interaction of war and society. Books on the relationship of law and statecraft have a tendency to be both dull and expensive, but Michael Howard's *The Laws of War: Constraints on Warfare in the Western World* (Yale UP, 1995) is a merciful exception, although now getting dated. *International Law and New Wars* by Christine Chinkin and Mary Kaldor (CUP, 2017) is more recent. Lawrence Freedman's *The Future of War: A History* (Penguin, 2018) is really about how we predict the evolution of conflict, and often how we fail to, and is therefore a useful corrective to all the speculation.

CHAPTER 3

Soldiering-plus and Gig Geopolitics

When the Somali Civil War led to the collapse of the state in the 1990s, its national waters were open for illegal fishing by outsiders on an industrial scale. Fish stocks dwindled and Somali fishing communities found themselves without livelihoods at the very time there was no effective central government either to support or to constrain them. At first, they banded together to form armed patrols in the hope of deterring foreign trawlers. Soon, though, they realised that a handful of men with AK-47 rifles and an RPG-7 grenade launcher, together costing maybe $1,000 on the local black market, could board and seize an unarmed merchant vessel with a multi-million-dollar cargo and hold it to ransom. Somalia's long coastline wraps around the Horn of Africa, past which runs one of the most heavily trafficked maritime trade routes in the world, connecting the Indian Ocean, the Arabian Peninsula and, through the Suez Canal, the Mediterranean. It accounts for almost 20 per cent of world trade and shipping. Targets were plentiful: in 2008, a reported 40 ships were seized and each *ransomed for between $500,000 and $2 million. Ships began sailing farther from the coast; the pirates fitted out trawlers as long-range motherships for their fast boats. Ships began being equipped with anti-boarding barbed wire and panic rooms, with the ability to deploy fire hoses and even carrying armed guards. By 2011, the problem was costing up to $6.9 billion in delayed deliveries and pricier shipping.*

So in came the navies of dozens of nations with too much to lose: multinational Combined Task Forces 150 and 151, the European Union's Operation Atalanta, and deployments by China, India and Russia. Even Japan, long unwilling to deploy out of area, sent ships from its Maritime Self-Defense Force. The methods used varied dramatically. The Russians caused a furore in 2010 when marines from the destroyer Marshal Shaposhnikov freed the hijacked MV Moscow University, a Liberian-flagged Russian tanker. The pirates were set adrift in an inflatable boat, with food and water but no navigation equipment, 300 nautical miles (560 km) at sea, where they likely perished. However it was done, though, the operations were largely successful. By 2013, the level of piracy had declined by more than 90 per cent.

Soldiers have never just been soldiers, after all. They have built roads and filled ditches. They have rescued climbers buried in avalanches and children stranded by floods. They have dazzled visiting dignitaries with their drill and shown off the latest military kit for potential buyers. They have distracted the population with choreographed pageantry or artfully staged pyrotechnics. These days, they variously repel or rescue migrants in their rickety boats and divert at-risk adolescents from lives in street gangs or on the dole. In the coronavirus pandemic of

2020, British soldiers dispensed masks, gowns and testing kits to hospitals, Spanish paratroopers enforced curfews on the streets of Madrid and army trucks emblazoned 'From Russia with Love' brought Russian military doctors and decontamination systems to hard-hit Italian towns in a soft-power act of Kremlin 'viral diplomacy' that was as inspired as it was cynical. The way soldiers are drawn into so many different aspects of state policy and public need reflects the universalisation of security that, itself, is one of the preconditions for the weaponisation of everything. Soldiers can be drafted into all kinds of other roles in the name of security – and for the same reason, all kinds of other institutions and individuals can be deployed to 'do security'.

THE SWISS ARMY KNIFE

This is the problem when soldiers become the state's ultimate Swiss Army knife, the multi-function tool that can be pressed into every use. While they may sometimes resent this, in the modern age, armed forces are keenly aware of the need to demonstrate their value and relevance to justify the growing price tags on their hardware, through this 'soldiering-plus', as one British officer put it to me. By the same token, as states begin to adapt to the weaponisation of everything, they are becoming more imaginative in how they use their soldiers to protect, project and preserve their geopolitical influence. What this reflects, though, is the blurring of the lines not just between what is soldiering and what is not, but what is security and what is not – and what the right instruments are to defend state and society.

In his *Discourses on Livy* (1517), that Renaissance policy wonk, statesman and author Niccolò Machiavelli observed that 'gold will not always get you good soldiers, but good soldiers will always get you gold'. He was arguing his case against the usual practice of the time, of Italian city-states hiring mercenaries to do their fighting. After all, this frequently led to the rise of virtual protection rackets and also, often, singularly ineffective and unmotivated defenders. However, he had also hit on a very important way that the astute use of effective military power – 'good soldiers' – can certainly get you gold, or whatever other asset a nation craves. The age of openly conquering territories with lucrative assets and exploiting them at will may be over (Saddam Hussein's short-lived invasion of Kuwait in 1990 was probably the last such blatant land grab for money; Russia took Crimea for essentially political reasons), but there are all kinds of other ways of monetising your military might.

Thus, there are two interconnected processes at work in the modern age. On the one hand, the roles that soldiers play are multiplying, in part as notions of just what 'security' means become ever broader. From food supplies to mental health provision, stockpiles of petroleum to media literacy classes, everything seems to be being securitised. In part, this is sloppy thinking or shameless bandwagon-leaping, but as this book will hope to demonstrate, there is a very real truth to this concern that in the modern age pretty much everything can be weaponised. Sometimes, soldiers can and will be able to play their role in meeting these wider threats, although they often cannot or should not. A Swiss Army knife is a very fine instrument indeed, but if you insist on adding more and more tools to it, and take out the knife to make room for, say, a bonsai rake and a magnifying glass, arguably you miss the point. Often it is better to use a different gadget, one specifically designed for that job, and not ruin your Swiss Army knife at the same time.

There has been a simultaneous upsurge in the use of non-state agencies in the kind of security roles once seen as essentially the preserve of government institutions, from espionage to warfare. Outsourcing, offshoring, the gig economy – all these processes reshaping our economies are also manifesting themselves in geopolitics. To a degree, this is a return to older traditions, when empires could be garrisoned and policed by corporate armies (in 1800, the forces of the British East India Company were double the size of the entire British army, and their East Indiamen better appointed than the Royal Navy's men-of-war), when ambassadors were as often as not merchants rather than just civil servants, and when wars could be fought by pirate and bandit proxy. This is the modern world, one in which soldiers can find themselves supporting business, and business can find itself soldiering.

SOLDIERING-PLUS

Soldiers may fight fewer conventional state-to-state wars these days, but they have acquired all kinds of new roles, first of all as high-end adjuncts to the emergency services. In the Caribbean, the US and Royal Navies both do their best to interdict drug shipments, even as the cartels themselves evolve. In 1997, the unlikely trio of a Russian gangster-entrepreneur running a Miami night club, a high-end car dealer and Nelson 'Tony' Yester, a Cuban immigrant and underworld enforcer, actually tried to broker a $35 million deal to sell the Cali drug cartel a Soviet-era submarine. That deal fell through (even in the 'wild 1990s', Russian submarines weren't up on eBay), but since then, the cartels have been building their own.

Elsewhere, as discussed at the top of this chapter, navies are back to their old roles as pirate-hunters. Nor is this only a Somali problem – these days the growing threat is off West Africa, in the Gulf of Guinea, through which flows most of Europe's maritime trade, with over 200 incidents in 2020 alone. In the South China Sea and the Malacca and Singapore straits, piracy is also endemic, and the suspicion is that here Beijing may use counter-piracy operations also as a way to justify an increasing militarisation of these waters.

Soldiers are not only muscular cops of the sea, though. They are also medical personnel and disaster relief specialists, with military deployments from two dozen countries delivering aid, rescuing survivors, distributing food and setting up first aid stations after the 2004 Indian Ocean tsunami, or the 2011 earthquake and tsunami in Japan, or the devastating 2010 earthquake that left Haiti shattered, hungry and soon prey to cholera. Peacekeeping can also be power projection. In 1990, there were only five Chinese personnel in all the UN's peacekeeping missions around the world; by 2020, China was the tenth largest contributor in troops (and covered 15 per cent of the total UN peacekeeping budget). As much as anything else, this has been a way of telegraphing Beijing's new status as a global power, and also acquiring a greater stake in UN activities. Even more directly, the end of the 2020 Armenia–Azerbaijan war over the disputed territory of Nagorno-Karabakh was brokered by Moscow and is guaranteed by Russian peacekeepers. The war, and especially Turkey's role in backing Azerbaijan, seemed to undermine Russia's previous hegemony over the region. By inserting almost 2,000 mechanised troops, Moscow clawed back a measure of credibility and control. This is, after all, where humanitarianism, soft power and military capability intersect.

Ain't Gonna Study (Shooting) War No More

POLITICAL WARRIORS

When the Israelis raided deep into Uganda to free an airliner full of hostages from Palestinian hijackers in 1976, they not only wanted to free the hostages but were also eager to demonstrate their will and capacity to strike wherever necessary to deter future terrorism. When the British launched the 1897 Benin Expedition, they were out to avenge the deaths of an earlier, wholly unsanctioned invasion. That mission, in turn, had been trying to break a trade monopoly held by the Kingdom of Benin. So the British were not only seeking to demonstrate – again for deterrent reasons – that even when their citizens were in the wrong, no one had the right to kill them; they also had trade on their mind. Soldiers have always been powerful expressions of a state's political interests and priorities, and their use is as much as anything else a performative act of the theatre of force. In an age of political war, this becomes all the more important. There are all kinds of geopolitical 'gold' that your 'good soldiers' can get you, often without a single shot being fired in anger.

This is the age of soft power, of influencing other countries' actions through attraction ('we want to be like that country and want that country to like us'), legitimacy ('that country has the right values or is otherwise on the right side of history') or agenda-setting ('that country is asking the right questions'). Sending your soldiers abroad to stop genocide or protect the peace inevitably runs the risk of their being caught in the middle of intractable local vendettas. As the only true superpower – for the moment – the US is often involved in such delicate balances. When it set up its Africa Command (AFRICOM) in 2007–08, for example, the idea was precisely that it would not be a war-fighting structure so much as a hub of military soft power. The trouble is that in practice this frequently meant engaging in counter-terrorist operations against jihadists such as al-Shabaab in East Africa and Boko Haram in Nigeria. That, in turn, often meant working with authoritarian governments and inevitable 'collateral damage'. The US claims that in all the hundreds of airstrikes and commando operations it has launched, only two civilians died, but this is widely disputed. The jury is still out on whether AFRICOM can yet be considered a successful example of soft power through military means.

In fairness, these are usually not the best ways of making friends and influencing people. Soldiers are often rather better at 'hard power' coercion, even without actually fighting. It is worth turning back to Machiavelli. In his *The Prince* (1513) – a book that is more of a satire than the dictator's 'how to' guide most assume – he notes that 'a question arises: whether it be better to be loved than feared or feared than loved?' He answers his own question, asserting that 'one should wish to be both, but, because it is difficult to unite them in one person', if you have to choose, 'it is much safer to be feared than loved'. (Essentially because people are 'ungrateful, fickle, false, cowardly, covetous' and can't be trusted.) Interestingly, he adds that a prince must make sure that, while inspiring fear, he does not become hated: he has to be reliable, honest and transparent in his tyranny.

Armed forces are therefore also political instruments in the most basic and obvious way: as a source of fear. That is the essence of deterrence, of encouraging an enemy not to attack by making them dread the consequences, but there are more complex and modulated ways of wielding this psychological weapon in the age of political war. A parade can hide a threat behind pageantry and choreography, for example, but sometimes the menace is deliberately more obvious. Perhaps resigned to being considered the bad boys of the modern world and thus with least to lose, the Russians have been particularly assiduous proponents of what I've elsewhere called 'heavy-metal diplomacy', sending bombers skirting NATO airspace, even wargaming nuclear attacks on neighbours. As I discuss in Chapter 10, this kind of 'dark power' can itself be a thuggish form of coercive diplomacy carried out by the military.

BALANCE (SHEETS) OF POWER

There is a two-way process between military power and political influence. Some countries make money simply by allowing their citizens to be recruited by private military companies. For example, by 2016, mercenaries and armed guards had become Uganda's top export, worth even more than coffee to the national balance of payments, protecting international aid workers, businesspeople and US diplomats in hot spots around the world. However, this is also a sector in which government assets, from armies to territory, can be used to turn a financial or political profit.

Arguably, the main reason why Britain has so desperately tried to cling on to such far-flung and seemingly irrelevant tokens of empire as the islands of Ascension in the South Atlantic – 34 square miles of volcanic rock – and the Chagos off Mauritius – an atoll whose main resources are fish and coconuts – is as much as anything else because it knows other powers have an interest. Ascension was a vital staging post for the British expeditionary force in the 1982 Falklands War, but since then has been above all important for the presence of a NASA/US Air Force observatory, one of the four Global Positioning System ground stations, a European Space Agency tracking station and a GCHQ electronic intelligence-gathering facility that works in cooperation with the US's National Security Agency. As for the Chagos islands, one is now home to the massive US military base of Diego Garcia, a lynchpin of the American presence in the region. Strategic bombers from Diego Garcia flew sorties over Afghanistan and the Persian Gulf. Ships from Maritime Pre-Positioning Ships Squadron 2 out of Diego Garcia moved a brigade of marines to Saudi Arabia for the Gulf War. The cameras and telescopes of the Ground-Based Electro-Optical Deep Space Surveillance (GEODSS) system of the 20th Space Control Squadron track Russian and Chinese satellites. And all of this is done at a facility leased from the British and built by the Americans and yet to which the British have free access.

More directly, the Republic of Djibouti is a small, under-developed country scarcely bigger than the state of New Jersey, and yet its strategic location on the Red Sea and the Bab-el-Mandeb Strait means it is a good place for a naval base. The French built one there (leasing it to the Americans), then the Italians and the Japanese. Rents on these bases account for more than 5 per cent of Djibouti's total GDP, and the decision to allow China to construct one of its own has also been leveraged to get them to build a new commercial port. China's military bought influence by spending in Djibouti; Djibouti used other countries' strategic interests to make a profit.

Countries themselves may act as mercenary companies in their own right. At the start of 2020, there were over 90,000 soldiers committed as 'blue helmets' on various UN peace-keeping missions. The six countries that provided the most were

Pakistan, India, Nepal, Rwanda, Bangladesh and, at the top of the league, Ethiopia. In terms of GDP per capita, according to the International Monetary Fund, Ethiopia is the poorest of that list, ranking 161st out of 186 countries. Is it, by contrast, world leader in altruism? Not so much. The UN pays a flat fee of around $1,500 per soldier per month, but to the state providing the force, not the individual grunt on the ground. That would not cover the basic pay and provisions of a British Army private but compares very favourably with an Ethiopian average salary of $275 per month, and the government can pocket the difference between what the UN provides and what it pays its men. Meanwhile, Ethiopia also gets useful training and experience for its troops and influence over what may be local conflicts – in this case in neighbouring Sudan and South Sudan.

Scaling up, when Iraq invaded Kuwait and neighbours such as Saudi Arabia and the UAE feared they might be next, they were happy to see the US-led multinational coalition deal with the problem. Doubly so, as many of these countries either lacked the forces to make a substantial contribution or – as in Saudi Arabia's case – the desire to do any fighting. So instead they stumped up direct payments of $84 billion to the US, Britain and France, who did the lion's share of the fighting, and extra support to cover bases and logistics. No one would suggest that the combatant countries actually made a profit on the war, or that they were motivated by the payments. Nonetheless, the way that rich but militarily weak or self-indulgent nations could simply outsource the violence – and the dying – to foreigners is a pattern that Machiavelli would have recognised from the days when mercenary captains fought Italian city-states' wars for them.

OUTSOURCING WAR

When is a mercenary not a mercenary, though? In 2015, as Russian warplanes joined the civil war in Syria, news emerged of a new fighting force on the ground: the Wagner Group private military company. While mercenary organisations are banned by law in Russia (and so it was reportedly registered in Argentina), Wagner was being run out of St Petersburg, had a training camp actually on the grounds of a Russian military base and was surprisingly well funded, able to recruit the pick of recently demobilised paratroopers, *Spetsnaz* special forces and similar elite veterans. Wagner became the tip of the spear in the Syrian government's fightback against the rebels.

By 2017, though, something had changed. Wagner no longer was able to offer top dollar (or rouble) and thus wasn't recruiting and retaining quite the same quality fighters. It also was no longer fielding the best kit. Suddenly, it was in negotiations with Damascus for a deal whereby it would receive a share in the profits from any oil and gas fields it reconquered. This proved a fateful step, the first on the path that took it to the contested region of Deir ez-Zor in February 2018. It was part of a joint force seeking to capture oil fields there, apparently not knowing or caring that there were US forces alongside the rebels, and this led to the monumental defeat mentioned in Chapter 1. Wagner scaled down its operations in Syria but soon started popping up across the world, from Venezuela to Mozambique, but now overtly making deals with local governments rather than being hired by Moscow.

So what had happened? When Wagner first deployed to Syria, it was simply a deniable arm of the Russian state. Above all, this meant deniable at home: the Kremlin knew that there

55

was no enthusiasm among the Russian population for risking their boys' lives in a distant country for an unpleasant regime. Wagner could provide the necessary assault troops to stiffen the Syrians' backbones but was technically a purely commercial venture, working for Damascus. No need for official announcements and military funerals when any of them died. Nothing to see here. That worked, but by 2017 the Russian military felt it didn't need what they saw as the cocky, undisciplined and overpaid Wagner contractors anymore.

But the Kremlin thought that Wagner might still be of use elsewhere. Part of the façade of Wagner's status as a private company had been its management by a businessman named Evgeny Prigozhin. Now he was entrusted with keeping Wagner up and running in case the Kremlin needed to use it again. Maintaining a mercenary company isn't cheap, and Prigozhin looked for new revenue streams, hence the contract that led to Deir ez-Zor. In other words, a fake mercenary company became a more real one – with the understanding that it might become a deniable front organisation again in the future. In the modern world, so many actors are protean, changeable, playing multiple roles and responding often to multiple masters.

Of late, the mercenary is coming back into vogue. Initially, they rebranded as private military company (PMC) contractors – not quite 'mercs', in that they generally do not engage in direct combat operations, but they do do everything short of it, from guarding facilities and running supply convoys to flying reconnaissance missions and training allies. It's now a global industry worth over $100 billion and increasingly essential to many modern conflicts. In the 1990s, there were some 50 government soldiers for every contractor; within a decade the ratio had closed to 10 to 1, thanks above all to the wars in Afghanistan and

Iraq. Indeed, at the sharp end, this ratio is even more striking: at peak in both wars, it was roughly one and a half contractors to every US soldier in-theatre.

In that context, it was perhaps inevitable that governments would begin to apply the same principles to war-fighting as to photocopier maintenance, prison building and street cleaning. In the outsourced wars of the Italian Renaissance, the mercenary captains were called *condottieri*, from *condotta*, contract. So too, today's battlefields are increasingly shaped by the contractors. This is the age of companies such as the infamous US behemoth Blackwater that seemed to adopt a policy of renaming itself whenever scandals reached a critical mass, becoming Xe and then rebranding again as Academi (who knows what it may be called by the time this book comes out). For instance, Kellogg, Brown & Root, a division of the American multinational Halliburton, was by 2005 the largest private military contractor in Iraq. For this, Uncle Sam paid a reported $13 billion. Even allowing for inflation, this is equivalent to the combined cost of the American Revolution, the War of 1812, the Mexican–American War and the Spanish–American War.

Even the UN hires private security companies to protect its missions. In 1994, when genocide was being practised with murderous abandon in Rwanda and no governments seemed inclined to step in, the UN's then-Undersecretary-General for Peacekeeping, Kofi Annan, considered hiring one of the biggest, DSL, to intervene. He ultimately hung back, saying that 'the world may not be ready to privatise peace', but it certainly seems to be willing again to privatise war.

While so far Western PMCs still play support rather than combat roles, Russia has blazed a trail that other opportunistic nations are following. In Libya, Turkey and Russia have both deployed hired fighters from Syria in support of rival factions in its civil war. Iran raised a force of Afghans to fight in Syria. The Black Shields Security Company in the UAE hired Sudanese mercenaries to fight in the Yemen civil war. Turkey sent Syrian mercenaries to fight for Azerbaijan in its 2020 war with Armenia.

The West may feel it is above such methods, but it is worth asking just how different this is to its time-honoured tactic of arming and paying local proxies, whether rebels in Syria or tribal militias in Iraq. The age of the *condottiere* is arguably back. An open question is quite what China will do as its geopolitical agenda becomes more assertive. As it drives its Belt and Road Initiative of infrastructure development, leveraged buyouts and dangerously generous loans deep through Asia and Europe and into Africa, involving sixty-five countries and almost $1 trillion of planned investments, this 'new Silk Road' is being guarded by an increasingly organised and active array of PMCs of its own. Chinese law bars them from using weapons abroad, but they have been seen with guns, nonetheless. Rapidly growing companies such as China Security & Protection, the Shandong Huawei Security Group and the rather alarmingly named Genghis Security Services not only are themselves often closely tied to Beijing's military and security apparatus, but so too are many of their clients. As one former British intelligence officer put it to me, 'Chinese corporations are ultra-capitalist organisations that nonetheless ultimately all work for the Communist Party'. And bit by bit, they are arming.

GIG GEOPOLITICS

Outsourcing goes beyond direct warfare and into non-kinetic contests. This century has also seen the explosion of the gig economy: individual freelancers and temporary workers, sometimes recruited directly, sometimes through online platforms or third-party matchmakers. It may seem ridiculous to draw comparisons with the cycle-courier who brings you your pizza, but this is less fanciful than might appear in an age when conflicts may be fought through the medium of carefully curated newspaper articles highlighting a grievance or attacking a government, and when online 'influencers' can pivot from hyping a hair product to pushing a political cause. This may be an age of multinational corporations, mass social movements and powerful governments – but a coincidence of technological, social and political change means that it is also the age of the individual. And many of them are for hire.

Suddenly, the world is full of people who seem to be doing the work of states, yet not as direct employees, nor even out of ideological commitment or patriotic passion. Journalists hired to write hit pieces; scholars saying the right things for a grant; think tanks producing recommendations to order. There may be no geopolitical equivalent of Uber yet, but lobbying, strategic communications (were I a cynic, I would suggest that this is what we call propaganda when we do it ourselves) and similar consultancy and service companies often act as the middlemen.

When dissident Saudi journalist Jamal Khashoggi walked into his country's embassy in Turkey in October 2018, he was grabbed by Saudi security officers, smothered and cut to pieces with a bone saw. A tragedy for Khashoggi, but a bonanza for the global network to whom Crown Prince Mohammed Bin Salman turned in a bid to head off the inevitable wave of horror and revulsion. In the next year, Riyadh spent an estimated $20 million on PR, lobbying and reputation management, much of which went to companies that, in turn, hired notionally independent experts, journalists and commentators willing to play up the prince's alleged reformist credentials, gloss over the murder as an aberration, highlight the importance of keeping Riyadh as a Western ally and generally fight the not-so-good information fight in the narrative battlegrounds of the world.

OUTSOURCING ESPIONAGE

Much espionage has always been outsourced. Rather than the suave James Bond or remorseless Jason Bourne, sipping cocktails before infiltrating an enemy base, the classic human intelligence case officer is essentially a recruiter and handler, someone whose job is – to put it at its bluntest – to make friends with foreigners and get them to betray their country. The case officer is usually working undercover in an embassy and protected by diplomatic immunity. The assets, the locals he or she recruits, are the ones doing the actual spying: copying documents, overhearing conversations or whatever else is required. (And they, depending on the kind of country they are working in, are the ones running the risk of anything from prison to a bullet in the back of the head.)

As with warfare, the actual job of being a case officer – and, indeed, running whole intelligence networks – was once often a specialised art practised by an array of gifted amateurs, trusted cohorts and international hirelings. As states became bureaucratised and professionalised, this increasingly became a job for civil servants, but here too outsourcing has crept back. Perhaps this was inevitable as it has also become increasingly technical, with satellites, spy ships, phone taps and electronic intercepts supplemented and overshadowed by the exponential rise of cellular communications and cyberespionage. Besides, for the US in particular, when the 9/11 attacks generated a sudden and irresistible demand for intelligence support for the 'War on Terror', this was the only way an intelligence community that had suffered a decade of contraction could respond rapidly. You cannot train officers to speak Farsi or pivot them from Kyiv to Kabul overnight, but you can hope to hire that existing expertise. Short-term response became long-term dependency, though: as a 2007 presentation from the Office of the Director of National Intelligence put it, 'We can't spy . . . if we can't buy!'

Already by then, 70 per cent of the US intelligence budget was going to private contractors. Much was technical, from building secure IT systems to collecting phone data. A lot was and still is analysis, though. (The infamous Edward Snowden worked inside the NSA as an analyst on contract from Booz Allen Hamilton, one of the big beasts in the US intelligence business.) Of course, analysis now is a term which can be stretched from writing reports about Chinese politics or the Bolivian economy, to targeting drone strikes based on studying surveillance feeds or finding vulnerabilities in foreign computer networks. Even human intelligence is out for contract. At peak, most US intelligence activity in Afghanistan was handled by 'green badge' contractors rather than government 'blue badge' spooks; so were more than three-quarters of the interrogations at the notorious Abu Ghraib prison in Iraq.

This is especially a feature of the US intelligence community, given its global ambitions, but not exclusive to them. After all, why not from time to time take advantage of the rise of a growing private intelligence sector? Many countries outsource intelligence analysis to international specialists. Technical espionage firms such as Israel's NSO Group and Italy's (subtly named) Hacking Team provide governments such as Saudi

Arabia, Togo, Venezuela and even Spain with the capacity to listen to dissidents' calls and hack into messaging abroad. The UAE hired ex-NSA hackers to target a critical journalist in the UK. In the 1990s, the Russian government hired Kroll Associates to track moneys embezzled as the Soviet Union collapsed, unable or unwilling to rely on its own intelligence services, as the old KGB was at the heart of this industrial-scale theft.

Elsewhere, the outsourcing is even more shadowy. As will be discussed in Chapter 6, the Russian intelligence services are increasingly turning to their comrades in the underworld, contracting them for jobs including assassination in Europe and the extraction of agents on the run. The burgeoning hacking field is another source of criminal outsourcing, and not only for the Russians. Arguably this is the perfect example of an activity where state spookery, outsourcing to corporate entities – whether licensed companies or transnational crime networks – and the gig economy, individuals picking up a job here, a task there, collide and combine.

And this is the point. Just as the growing transformation of the military as the state's Swiss Army knife epitomises the way the notions of conflict and security are changing, so too does the widening remit for outsourced guardians and champions of its interests. As the next chapters will explore, from soldiers to hackers, spin-doctors to gangsters, lawyers to accountants, states now have so many 'good soldiers' they can deploy in their struggles with others. Some may work directly for it, but most are the pieceworkers, subcontractors and day-labourers of the modern conflict industry in all its many forms. In the process, the clear demarcations of command and control, authority and responsibility, get blurred. Offensives can as easily be launched from a newsroom or boardroom as a cabinet war-room. Your 'soldiers' may not carry your passport; they may not even know they are in a war, or on whose side they are fighting.

WANT TO KNOW MORE?

On the dogs of war, Sean McFate's *The Modern Mercenary* (OUP, 2015) in many ways picks up where P.W. Singer's *Corporate Warriors* (Manas, 2005) ends. *Outsourced Empire: How Militias, Mercenaries, and Contractors Support US Statecraft* by Andrew Thomson (Pluto, 2018) is a sharp, critical assessment of the outsourcing of governance as well as war-fighting. John Hillen's *Blue Helmets: The Strategy of UN Military Operations* (Brassey's, 2000) is a little dated but still the basic text on this topic. Andrew Palmer's *The New Pirates* (I.B. Tauris, 2014) and Jay Bahadur's more personal *The Pirates of Somalia* (Pantheon, 2011) are good on the maritime side of things.

PART II

Business, and Other Crimes

CHAPTER 4

Business

Palau is a tropical archipelago of more than 500 islands in the Philippine Sea, known for its turquoise lagoons, emerald rainforests and shimmering beaches, and with one of the lowest crime rates in the world. It is not normally considered a warzone. But this is exactly what it became in 2017, albeit as an economic warzone, when its government had the temerity to reject Beijing's demands that it break ties with Taiwan. The mainland government has, after all, for years conducted an aggressive diplomatic offensive to delegitimise the very notion of there being an independent Republic of China. As a precondition for any nation to have diplomatic relations with Beijing, it requires the breaking of any formal relationship with Taipei. Most countries – including the US and European nations – have meekly accepted these terms, sidestepping them by establishing 'trade offices' and 'cultural offices' in Taiwan that are essentially diplomatic missions that dare not speak their name. Tiny Palau, though, was one of just seventeen countries in the world which had not yet acknowledged Beijing's 'One China' claim to

Taiwan. This could not, would not be accepted by the increasingly self-confident masters of the mainland.

In the preceding few years, Palau had attracted the attention of the growing numbers of affluent Chinese looking to holiday in the sun. In 2010, fewer than 1,000 Chinese visited these Micronesian islands – by 2015, it was over 90,000, more than half of the total number of tourists. The smallest country in the world, with a population of just 20,000, Palau is heavily dependent on tourism, which accounts for almost 45 per cent of its GDP. No wonder that Beijing thought it had identified a target of opportunity.

In November 2017, Chinese package tour operators were forced to stop selling trips to Palau. Indeed, the formidable engines of state censorship actually made the very word 'Palau' disappear from the Chinese internet, if anyone tried to search for it. The number of visitors dropped by half; hotels and restaurants that had hurriedly been built to cater for the boom found themselves empty; and charter airlines closed. Taiwan provides more than $10 million in aid every year – the price of continued diplomatic recognition – but this was just a fraction of the revenue lost by China's quiet blockade.

Nor was this a one-off. When Seoul agreed to provide a base for the US THAAD missile defence system in 2016, an angry Beijing imposed another package holiday ban, which cost South Korea $6.5 billion in nine months. Mysteriously enough, a whole series of alleged breaches of fire and safety codes were also suddenly discovered in Korean businesses in China. Three-quarters of the supermarkets run by Lotte, on whose land the THAAD batteries were to be sited, were closed or otherwise affected. It is a mark of the dark side of the globalised economy when even tourism and supermarkets can be weaponised.

THE EMBARGO

The concept of the embargo has a long history – the word likely comes from the Latin *imbarricare*, to bar something closed, to barricade it. However, it was only with the expansion and regularisation of trade that it became possible to see constraining it as a weapon of war. Rome tried to embargo Carthage in the third century BC; at the Third Lateran Council of 1179, Pope Alexander III banned trade with the 'Saracens'; in the fourteenth century, Venice tried to break the Ottoman Empire by blockading Egypt. The idea was to strangle the empire's lucrative trade in Indian spices and starve its shipyards of the timber, iron and pitch they needed. As it was, though, it was too easy and too profitable to break these embargoes. In the twentieth century, Soviet leader Joseph Stalin would ask contemptuously how many divisions had the Pope; in the twelfth, the question was, how many war galleys could the Papacy deploy?

It was really only in the fifteenth century that states began to acquire new powers to control and constrain business, and barter and cash-on-the-barrel trade increasingly became supplemented by that revolutionary new concept, the letter of credit. The beginnings of a modern economy brought with it the beginnings of modern economic warfare. In the past, powers such as the Venetians and the Ottomans could blockade a rival's ports and trade routes with their ships and their soldiers, but smugglers slipped past under cover of night and traders bribed their way through checkpoints. Now, though, trade could be throttled and a country's exchequer drained by judicious manipulation of licensing and credit. As Andrea Contarini, the combative Doge of Venice, gleefully noted, 'our city's wealth and mercantile vigour have become as powerful as our ships and our Arsenal'.

In the seventeenth and eighteenth centuries, the main instrument of economic warfare was privateering, unleashing sanctioned pirates against an enemy's merchant shipping. The English enthusiastically adopted this tactic in the First Anglo–Dutch War (1652–54). One Dutch ambassador presciently said that 'the English are about to attack a mountain of gold; we are about to attack a mountain of iron'. Ultimately, the iron of British sea power was able to bite off quite a lot of Dutch gold in the form of convoys seized by their privateers: more than a thousand merchant ships, all told. This was a double-edged sword, though. During the 1654–60 Anglo–Spanish War, privateers took more than 1,500 English merchant ships, and British trade routes would be harried in subsequent conflicts, until the Royal Navy was able to stamp its dominance on the seaways and the 1708 Cruisers and Convoys Act saw warships protecting its shipping. (Just as well, as the end of the War of Spanish Succession saw many British privateers returning to old-fashioned piracy.)

GLOBALISATION'S STING

In 1806, Napoleon imposed his Continental System, forbidding European nations from trading with the UK, which he apocryphally is meant to have called 'a nation of shopkeepers'. Of course, Britain was also a nation of merchants, seamen and smugglers, and in any case many European economies depended far more on Britain's markets than vice versa. Neither French warships nor French customs officers could enforce the embargo.

After all, by the nineteenth century, international economics was becoming a battleground, but one fought increasingly through laws and regulations rather than domesticated pirates on the high seas. The US Embargo Act of 1807 was a general ban on all foreign trade, intended to try and keep the country out of the Napoleonic Wars, not least as the British had a habit of seizing American ships and press-ganging their sailors under the questionable pretext that they had been 'born British'. It failed, because US commercial interests saw their profits at stake. A measure ironically intended to avert foreign wars arguably helped pave the way for the Anglo–American War of 1812. But this was nonetheless significant precisely because it marked the emergence of a clear notion that economic war could be considered not an adjunct to a regular shooting war – as Napoleon's Continental System blockade was intended – but as an alternative. This is exactly the kind of calculation present in American scholar-diplomat George Kennan's vision of political warfare, and in today's Russian security thinking, for example.

It was really in the twentieth century that sanctions and embargoes came into their own. Even during the Cold War, when the capitalist West and – officially – socialist Soviet bloc ostensibly espoused different economic systems and existed in different economic spheres, this was not so cut and dried. One of the reasons for the savage collectivisation campaigns of the early Stalin era, when land was in effect nationalised and peasants forced into becoming serfs of the state, was because the Soviets wanted to sell the capitalists grain. The money was then spent on expertise and machinery for industrialisation. Later, it would be gold, oil and gas that would flow to the West, in return for industrial equipment and, in an ironic turnaround, grain to feed a hungry Soviet population.

Soviet commissars and Western capitalists may have affected to despise each other, but the Moscow Narodny Bank, based right in the City of London financial district, acquired a reputation for professionalism and punctiliousness. They had to, given the scrutiny under which a British-based and Soviet-owned bank laboured, and given Moscow's need to connect to the global capital markets. Meanwhile, since 1950, Western countries had been maintaining a strategic technologies and materials embargo on the Soviet bloc under the auspices of COCOM, the Coordinating Committee for Multilateral Export Controls. While there was a certain degree of spying and smuggling – the Soviet intelligence and security agency, the KGB, would get quite good at this – nonetheless, this not only helped keep the West's overall (and growing) technological lead, but also emphasised how far the two blocs' economic spaces were overlapping.

The more the world's economies become interconnected and interdependent, the more vulnerable they become. Turkey may be a member of NATO, but its produce graces the shelves of Russian supermarkets and its beaches have become a popular holiday destination for Russians looking for some Mediterranean sun. As already mentioned, when a Turkish fighter shot down a Russian bomber close to the border with Syria at the end of 2015, Moscow banned the import of Turkish fruit and vegetables and the sale of charter holidays, the latter alone being worth $3.5 billion a year. Likewise, the Venezuelan regime may denounce the US as run by an 'extremist sector of the white supremacists of the Ku Klux Klan', and Washington reciprocate by saying its leader, Nicholás Maduro, is running a 'devastating dictatorship'. Nonetheless, in 2018, their mutual trade was worth $24.2 billion – about a quarter of Venezuela's total GDP. Indeed, Venezuela held $5.5 billion in US shares and other investments. Thus, it was particularly vulnerable when Washington imposed sweeping new measures limiting Venezuela's access to US financial markets. To be sure, corruption and mismanagement have played a greater role than any embargoes, but in 2019, Venezuela's economy shrank by 35 per cent and inflation hit 20,000 per cent.

Sanctions and embargoes also became expressions of social moods and movements. Apartheid South Africa, Israel, Pinochet's Chile: at different times, political actors have been able to galvanise public opinion to boycott imports from these countries, push for divestment, even cancel cultural and sporting links. Sometimes these have their impacts – apartheid South African minister Piet Koornhof admitted that 'play and sport are strong enough to cause political and economic relations to flourish or collapse' – but the real bite of any sanctions come in their economic costs.

BUT DO SANCTIONS WORK?

This helps explain why states – especially richer ones, or those with a particular resource in demand – are tempted to turn to economic statecraft, which is often a delicate way of describing economic wars fought through sanctions, boycotts and the manipulation of currencies. It plays to their strengths. It is ostensibly bloodless (although, as will be discussed in Chapter 7, the real toll can be catastrophic). It can either be played up as a heroic struggle or played down as a tedious matter of customs controls and procedure, as political circumstances dictate. There is just one irksome little question: do sanctions actually work?

When Russia annexed Crimea, this became a battle of wills: Moscow's 'little green men' on the ground versus Western sanctions. Individuals associated with the invasion were barred from travel to the West and their assets frozen. Trade specifically with Crimea was banned. As of writing, seven years on, the Russian tricolour still flutters over Crimea.

Then Moscow went further, stirring up a proxy war in south-eastern Donbas. Again, unable or unwilling to deploy military force, the West turned to sanctions. Supplying dual-use technologies (civilian ones which also may have a military value), long- and mid-term loans to state banks and support for Russian oil and gas exploration and exploitation were all restricted. Again, as of writing, that messy, low-level conflict is still rumbling on.

It is not that these sanctions had no effect. Just not enough. According to the International Monetary Fund, between 2014 and 2018, all they did was slow the *growth* of the Russian economy by 0.2 per cent each year, costing it around a trillion roubles ($15 billion). That was not trivial, but nor was it sufficient to force Vladimir Putin to back down, something that would have been politically disastrous for him. The bottom line is that Crimea and to a degree Ukraine matter much more to Russia than to the West. Besides, the cost goes both ways: according to a UN Special Rapporteur, EU countries lost almost $40 billion dollars a year thanks to the sanctions and Russian counter-sanctions. Admittedly, this is a much smaller proportion of the total EU economy, but that the measures cost Russia less than the EU should give us pause. In any case, if the situation looked truly desperate, Putin could have escalated in old-fashioned or new-fangled ways that played to his strengths: holding Ukraine to ransom under peril of full-scale invasion, or a campaign of terrorist violence and destructive cyberattack, even going further than he did in cutting off oil and gas supplies before the cold winter. Given all that, it is hard to see how economic sanctions could have hit that sweet spot between being damaging enough to compel policy change and so disastrous that they force the other side to escalate.

After all, sanctions can worsen a situation. In 1940–41, in the so-called ABCD Encirclement, the Americans, British, Chinese and Dutch barred sales of crucial oil, iron and steel to Japan as a response to its aggression in China and Indochina. What was intended as a warning and a rebuff to Japanese militarism arguably accelerated them on the path to Pearl Harbor. Japanese nationalists considered the embargo an affront, and cooler heads realised how vulnerable their country was, so long as it could be denied these essential industrial resources. Strategic planners turned to measures to guarantee access to these vital war-fighting resources, such as the oil fields of the Dutch East Indies – something that they knew would require taking on the US.

When sanctions do work, the trick is often to make the objective sufficiently specific and limited that it is worth the other side complying. Otherwise, they tend at best simply to freeze a situation, preventing things from worsening, but not fixing the basic issue. After a mob invaded the US embassy in Tehran in 1979 during the Iranian Revolution, taking 52 hostages, Washington froze $12 billion in assets held abroad and imposed a trade embargo. Just over a year later, the sanctions were lifted when the hostages were freed. That's a good result, but the key point is that Washington was able to bring pressure to bear that was disproportionate to any value the hostages had to the Iranian revolutionary regime, and with a political cost of compliance that was bearable for Tehran. Contrast that with the ongoing saga of Iran's nuclear weapons programme. The US began placing sanctions on Iran in a bid to block its nuclear programme – which it claims is purely for civilian purposes, but with neither great conviction nor persuasiveness – in 1995. In 2006, this was expanded multinationally under a UN mandate, covering everything from banking transactions to technology transfers. In 2015–16, a provisional agreement lifted most sanctions in return for limited Iranian concessions, but the US reinstated theirs in 2018, in part because of Tehran's adventurism in the Middle East, but also because of continued suspicion that it was pursuing a military nuclear capability (and also, in fairness, because the ever-erratic Trump administration was looking for a fight).

Twenty-five years on, after a swingeing series of sanctions and embargoes that have cost it some $100 billion in lost oil revenues and potential foreign investment (and perhaps 5 times as much when second-order costs and impacts are considered) and inflation often topping 25 per cent a year, Iran is no less active in its foreign operations, no less hostile to the West and, above all, seemingly no less committed to developing the nuclear weapons that it regards as its only true guarantee of national security. Its programme has suffered serious setbacks and much of it was dismantled in order to secure the 2016 deal. What has been dismantled can be reassembled, though, and according to the International Atomic Energy Agency, by 2020, Iran had nearly tripled its stockpile of enriched uranium, with the capability to enrich it to 60 per cent: well beyond the 4 per cent levels needed for nuclear power stations and 20 per cent for medical isotopes, and close to the levels required for a bomb.

The truth seems to be that sanctions can hurt a country but rarely bring it to its knees. This is especially true of authoritarian states, which can generally absorb much more economic pain, simply by transferring it to their populations and either suppressing any consequent discontent or even using it to whip up 'rally round the flag' nationalism. When key cronies of Putin were personally sanctioned after Crimea, their losses were covered by the Russian treasury. In effect, mega-rich Russians whose wealth was often largely already stolen from the Russian people were compensated with money that could otherwise have been spent on public health or education. At the same time, the state media machine presented the sanctions as evidence of Western 'Russophobia', spurious evidence to support Putin's new narrative that the country needed to be a fortress, disciplined and united to face this unwarranted foreign interference. And worst of all, the West generally knows this. The day after delivering an elegant and eloquent defence of sanctions against Russia because of its annexation of Crimea, a British diplomat privately admitted to me 'of course they are not going to change the situation on the ground. But politicians want to do something, and this is something. Sanctions are . . . public, straightforward. The government can look tough.'

That's as nothing to North Korea's situation. It has been under US sanctions in some form or another since the 1950s, and UN and EU ones since 2006. Its rulers appear willing to resist to the last ordinary North Korean, though. More than 40 per cent of North Koreans suffer from malnutrition, but thanks to workarounds and smuggling tricks, the use of organised crime (discussed in Chapter 6) and brutal repression of the population, the state survives – and its rulers prosper. Previous 'Supreme Leader' Kim Jong-il reportedly spent almost a million dollars a year smuggling in cognac for himself and his cronies. His son, Kim Jong-un, enjoys his 200-foot luxury yacht, described by his friend the US basketball player Dennis Rodman as a 'cross between a ferry and a Disney boat', valued at $8 million. If the alternative is death, prison or powerlessness, then you will do what you have to do to stay in power.

Many of the claimed successes of international sanctions tend to be about appearances rather than realities. Poorer countries' regimes may tidy up their act in a way that satisfies the West, but they will try to find loopholes. Honduras was sanctioned by the US after a military coup in 2009 toppled Manuel Zelaya's Liberal Party government. Five months later, sanctions were lifted after elections. That may sound like a success, but Zelaya was prevented from being able to contest the poll, which saw the election of rightist Porfirio Lobo Sosa, the generals' favoured candidate. A similar process took place in the Central African Republic. In 2003, François Bozizé staged a coup and the CAR was under sanctions, until 2005, after he had held elections and elected himself. Sanctions are by no means useless: they signal political disquiet in a very public way, they can target individuals believed to be specially involved in abuses, they impose costs on a regime. They have their place in the geopolitical toolbox. But by themselves, they are of questionable value, and the connection between economic might and political power is a more complex one than some advocates of the sanctions weapon suggest.

Indeed, they only represent part of the arsenal of economic warfare. At the other end of the spectrum there is 'economic guerrilla warfare': the use of cyberattacks, currency manipulations, flooding a country with counterfeit money and other covert or deniable dirty tricks. They are not necessarily intended to bring down the enemy, but weaken, infuriate, demoralise or destabilise through myriad paper cuts and pinpricks. For example, in May 2020, suspected Iranian hackers unsuccessfully attacked Israeli water purification plants. The next day, a cyber-attack crashed the systems regulating the flow of traffic to and from Iran's Shahid Rajaee port. The ensuing chaos left hundreds of trucks gridlocked outside the port and container ships stranded at sea, disrupting Iran's maritime trade for days. Israel, of course, denied everything, but with a nod and a wink to make sure Tehran understood the warning.

THE END OF US HEGEMONY

The age of overt imperialism is – largely – a thing of the past, even when it comes to economic warfare. Instead, we have informal empire: in the twenty-first century, the outsourcing of power is manifest in efforts to use a toxic mix of corruption, influence, promises and subterfuge to suborn whole national leaderships, supplemented often by direct economic leverage.

One would think that Washington held all the cards, not just because of the size of its economy – equivalent to more than the entire EU combined – but also its pivotal position in the world's financial system. SWIFT is a global network that allows banks to transfer money between each other (or technically not the money, but payment orders for it). While it is based in Belgium, there is increasing evidence not only that the US NSA monitors its transfer communications, but that Washington has exerted leverage on the network in the past. In 2012, it bowed to US pressure to disconnect most Iranian banks, and there are regular calls for the same to be done to Russia. Otherwise, the dollar still accounts for more than 60 per cent of all sovereign reserves and the keystones of the world's financial architecture are the US dollar clearing system and the Federal Reserve. Not just Washington's bank, the Fed is a crucial global source of liquidity in a crisis, and the metaphorical vault (because these days almost all money is a virtual commodity, a particular constellation of binary ones and zeros) where many other governments and financial institutions keep their reserves, too.

In the twenty-first century, Washington has shown itself increasingly willing to try to use this pivotal position for its own advantage. It doesn't just impose its own embargoes, it also employs secondary sanctions that cut off access to the very global financial system. Banks cannot work as they are used to if they cannot access the dollar clearing system, and companies and states can hardly raise extra capital. Enemies may be the targets, but allies find themselves dragooned into Washington's economic wars.

So far, so imperial. But again, we have to ask the basic question: is this working? Financial power, it turns out, isn't quite the same as military power. Countries willing to pay for the privilege of autonomy, or which see no alternative, can neutralise this kind of blunt economic power. Both Russia and China have made great strides to 'de-dollarise' their economies for this very reason. Between 2017 and 2020, for example, Moscow's holdings of US Treasury securities – essentially, US state debt – fell from $105 billion to just $3.8 billion. Russia has also set up SPFS, its alternative to SWIFT. While so far this is limited and very much a last-resort alternative, as it begins to connect with China's Cross-Border Inter-Bank Payments System, as well as other countries eager to acquire alternatives, it starts to erode the previous supremacy of SWIFT. Indeed, since 2019, Germany, France and the UK have also established INSTEX, a limited alternative of their own, to allow specific non-dollar trade with Iran to bypass Washington's efforts to force European countries to abide by US sanctions.

Besides which, just as in real war, there are risks in launching this kind of direct economic offensive. In an age of global trade and finance, where the world is wrapped in supply chains and multinational consortia, this has become vastly more dangerous, for everyone involved. Under Donald Trump, the US launched an off-and-on trade war with China. By the start of 2020, Washington had imposed tariffs on more than $360 billion of Chinese goods, from televisions to car parts, and Beijing retaliated with similar duties on more than $110 billion of American products. Who actually pays for this? In many cases, it is the consumer, and also often other countries connected in the same supply chains.

As of the time of writing, in the early months of the Biden presidency, it is still unclear whether the Chinese will be willing to make some concessions, especially over intellectual property – a key issue given their propensity to, if we are blunt, simply steal others' designs and innovations. If they do, it may count as a conditional win for the US, but it would be an expensive one that has hurt many and undermined Washington's status around the world.

THE NEW IMPERIALISTS?

The old conventional wisdom was that rich democracies could use economic means to bring evil despots to heel. This need not mean sanctions: Germany believed that *Wandel durch Handel*, 'change through trade', would make post-Soviet Russia reform away from authoritarianism as it became more enmeshed with Western economies. It looks as if this is the wrong way round. It is not just that authoritarians can use trade as a weapon themselves, but that overt sanctions are a very blunt instrument.

They can certainly weaken a country and contribute to its gradual decay. The classic example would be the slow-motion collapse of the Soviet Union, primarily laid low by its own economic inefficiencies, but exacerbated by both the pressure of trying to keep up with the US in the arms race and blocked access to modern technologies and investment capital. At best, though, this worked because the USSR was dying anyway – and it still all but bankrupted America.

The latest conventional wisdom, then, is that a new model of economic warfare is allowing a new imperial hegemon to emerge: China, rich, ambitious and increasingly looking beyond its borders to establish for itself a serious place in the world. There is much hyperbole about the Chinese Communist Party's alleged special advantages: its reputed ability to think and plan in terms of decades and generations, not just the next electoral cycle; its subtlety; its ruthless cynicism. It is hard not to suspect that that says more about Western stereotyping. The depressing truth is rather that beyond the incestuous interconnection of big business and government in China, Beijing's real advantages are foreign greed, short-termism and naivety.

The Chinese have been happy to splash the cash. Their Belt and Road Initiative (BRI), for example, is a massively ambitious infrastructure programme intended to link China to markets across the world, likely to cost well over a trillion dollars by 2028. As they build ports and power stations in Africa, roads and railways across Eurasia and even 'Ice Silk Road' shipping routes across northern seas as climate change melts the way for them, of course they are also trying to buy friends and influence people.

The US and other powers such as Australia, India and Japan with particular reason to watch Beijing's new assertiveness with alarm decry this as 'economic imperialism'. And yet, for many this is an offer difficult to refuse. The Chinese offer a lot of money, with – at least at first – seemingly few strings attached: no sanctimonious demands that their partners be democratic or transparent, no anti-corruption measures to stop local grandees from skimming their cut on the way. The strength of this approach is that it comes not with a glower and a stick, but a smile and an open hand – full of cash.

Because, of course, there are strings. Sometimes, it looks as if Beijing's largesse is intended to encourage other countries into debt-traps, for example. The obvious example is Sri Lanka's Magampura Mahinda Rajapaksa Port. Something of a white elephant project from the first, when Sri Lanka turned to Beijing for loans, it was happy to oblige, but stipulated that a Chinese company had to be lead constructor, using Chinese labourers. In effect, many of the billions Sri Lanka borrowed from China simply went right back to China. The port was never likely to be viable, and once opened in 2010, it sank more and more into the red. In 2017, it was leased to China for ninety-nine years in return for forgiveness of more debt. Many foreign analysts wondered, why would Beijing want to take over a loss-making port, were it not as part of a wider strategic agenda?

Maybe because it thinks it can make a going concern of it, when the Sri Lankans could not. In 2016, after all, the China Ocean Shipping Company took over Greece's struggling Piraeus Port and turned it into the second-largest maritime hub in the Mediterranean. In any case, even before COVID-19 shook up the global economy and knocked over the geopolitical chessboard, there were suggestions that, like other would-be hegemons before them, the Chinese were running up against some of the limitations of this kind of project, with its assumption that nations can be bought, rather than just rented. Many

BRI projects ended up unfinished, unproductive or embezzled into failure. Formerly eager partners were having second thoughts. From coal plants in Pakistan to an airport in Sierra Leone, a port in Myanmar to a road in Bangladesh, BRI projects worth billions have been scrapped or scaled down. Even seeming success stories, like the new rail links between China and Europe, are only being kept viable by subsidies from Beijing.

And these are likely to shrink, as the Chinese themselves seem to be questioning their strategy. Even before coronavirus, the once-inexorable rise of China's foreign investment had been slowing. More and more recipient countries are demanding proper and long-term investment rather than just loans, if Beijing wants to pay to play. Debts that essentially cycle straight back to China like the Sri Lankan port project are one thing, but proper long-term investment would tax even Beijing's burgeoning economy. Back in 2018, the deputy head of China's State Council's Development Research Centre admitted that there was already a $500 billion funding gap in the BRI.

Besides, what has all this really bought China? A port here and a factory there, to be sure, but arguably the natural workings of the market could have accomplished that. Formal acknowledgement of Beijing as the 'true' Chinese capital, but that is an easy enough concession for countries far from Asia and who anyway can maintain diplomatic relations with Taiwan through other means. One could argue that the Chinese are discovering what, in their day, the Americans, the Soviets, the French, the British, even the Romans discovered: empires are an expensive luxury, and while they may be meant for the benefit of the imperial power, they will often end up subverted by the notional subalterns. Of course, that doesn't mean that anyone enjoys or should appreciate the experience of imperialism. Rather, it is that the process often turns out less predictably positive for the imperialists. Arguably, a far more useful, pervasive and cost-effective form of imperialism is not conquest but economic subversion. Make the other country crave your goods and your capital. Give political and business leaders, opinion-shapers and trend-makers their own selfish reasons to follow your lead. Perhaps, as we will see in the next chapter, the lobbyist, the investor, the influencer and the corrupter have truly replaced the pith-helmeted conquerors of imperialism 1.0 and maybe even the sanctions and megaprojects of a short-lived imperialism 2.0?

WANT TO KNOW MORE?

There is a considerable literature on sanctions and economic warfare today, much of it quite partisan. Robert Blackwill's *War by Other Means: Geoeconomics and Statecraft* (Harvard UP, 2016) remains the standard, though *Shrewd Sanctions: Economic Statecraft in an Age of Global Terrorism* by Meghan O'Sullivan (Brookings, 2002), while narrower in focus, has some interesting points to make. As with most edited collections, Mikael Wigell, Sören Scholvin and Mika Aaltola's *Geo-economics and Power Politics in the 21st Century* (Routledge, 2020) is a mixed bag, but has some great chapters. Specifically on China, *Chinese Economic Statecraft: Commercial Actors, Grand Strategy, and State Control* by William Norris (Cornell UP, 2016) and *Belt and Road: A Chinese World Order* by Bruno Macaes (Hurst, 2018) are both worth reading.

CHAPTER 5

Buying Friends and Influencing People

'Surge forward, killing as you go, to blaze us a trail of blood!'

Which warlord, terrorist or gung-ho army commander issued this gory battle cry to his troops? It was actually, according to the Wall Street Journal, Ren Zhengfei, founder of the Chinese technology corporation Huawei. In 2018, he told the staff of its Hangzhou research and development centre that 'the company has entered a state of war' against the West: not just its business rivals, but the countries that dared refuse to deal with Huawei, too.

There is power to be won from monopolistic control of strategic assets. China, for example, controls most of the world's supply of the rare earths neodymium and dysprosium, used in advanced magnets and lasers. In its heyday in the 1970s, the OPEC cartel controlled more than half the world's oil production and thus had a significant influence on pricing. There is also power in monopolistic control of market segments (ask Google or Apple) as well as vital intellectual property.

The modern cliché that information is 'the new oil' may be irritating and a problematic analogy, but the technologies to share and process information, such as quantum computing and artificial intelligence, undoubtedly will be crucial sources of power in the future. However, actually using these assets to exert power is often difficult. Producers will look to alternative suppliers or ingredients. Companies cannot always be weaponised reliably, and rivals can quickly emerge. Data can be stolen. Arguably, real economic power is rather more subtle, to be found at the confluence of technology, investment and greed.

THE HUAWEI HINGE

Huawei may prove to be at a turning point. Its rise had previously seemed unstoppable, a metaphor representing the new China's capability to use a combination of genuine value, market strength, political connections and leveraged self-interest to buy an informal empire for itself. The company – its very name can be variously translated as 'China can' and 'splendid act' – has from the first been close to the state. To some, it is nothing less than a front company for the Chinese Communist Party, to others a business that understands when it needs to do favours for the government. But in many ways this very debate misses the point. China, like Putin's Russia and many other authoritarian-capitalist countries around the world, is a hybrid state, where the boundaries between public and private (and, some would suggest, legal and illegal) are mobile, porous, sometimes even meaningless.

Nonetheless, beyond the quality and value of its products, Huawei's rise abroad reflects the fact that whispering sweet promises of profit can be so much more effective than shouting threats of sanctions.

Founded in 1987, Huawei only opened offices in the UK and US in 2001, on the back of the telecommunications boom. Pretty much from the first, there were security concerns. Huawei not only had a track record of copying other people's technology, but there were fears that allowing it a stake in national telecommunications would open back doors for Chinese electronic espionage. While notionally independent, the $122 billion telecoms behemoth cannot operate without the state's indulgence, and some hundred of its senior employees are regarded by Washington as linked to the military or intelligence agencies. Ren Zhengfei himself is a former engineer in the Chinese military.

However, Huawei was competitive, nimble and very, very welcoming. In Britain, it wined and dined politicians and opinion-makers of every political shade, pumped millions into universities and engaged some of the most powerful lobbying and PR firms around. In 2015, it hired Lord Browne, the well-connected erstwhile head of oil firm BP and senior business adviser to former prime minister David Cameron, to chair its UK arm, and paid several other former senior civil servants and businesspeople to sit on its board as non-executive members, for upwards of £100,000 a year.

Perhaps even more powerfully, Huawei got local telecoms partners BT, Three and Vodafone hooked on its participation in their ambitious development plans. When the debate started about who should be at the heart of the roll-out of super-fast, super-rich 5G mobile data services, Huawei was perfectly positioned and had local companies themselves acting as its most ardent boosters. Faced with a serried phalanx of the 'great and the good' lobbying for Huawei, with the company itself promising to make the UK a world-beating 5G nation, at a bargain price, British prime minister Boris Johnson seemed convinced. He did not even seem concerned that an angry US was claiming that intelligence cooperation would be jeopardised as a result. Ren was reportedly jubilant. In characteristically military idiom, he compared it with the battle for Stalingrad in the Second World War, a battle that turned the tide against the Axis. This was not just one lucrative contract, but could be leveraged for other deals around the world.

Then things changed in 2020. Ironically, this may well have been due to the coronavirus pandemic, and Beijing's fury at the way that it was being blamed (albeit rightly) for being late and reluctant to tell the rest of the world about the threat coming out of Wuhan. When Australia called for an independent enquiry into the virus's origins, China retaliated with – surprise, surprise – economic sanctions. When the global debate turned to Beijing's failure to be wholly open about the outbreak, Chinese internet trolls and disinformation sites began broadcasting all kinds of toxic alternative narratives, suggesting even that the virus had been a US biological attack. Foreign countries that dared express concerns were taken to task by an undiplomatic array of 'wolf warrior' diplomats – taking their name from the patriotic action movies described in Chapter 10 – and threatened with sanctions.

It will likely prove to be a turning point in China's policies towards the outside world. China used the crisis as an excuse to impose new security laws on former British colony Hong Kong, in defiance of the terms of the handover. When London complained, Beijing threatened unspecified countermeasures. The debate shifted, and Huawei's critics were empowered. Depending on your perspective, Huawei was either caught in the crossfire or unmasked as the Chinese state proxy it always was, but either way, it began to be phased out of the UK's 5G project. Indeed, London is trying to put together a 'D10' consortium of democratic nations that could develop its own 5G technology to sideline Huawei altogether.

This is, of course, the story of just one company, one contract and one point in time. Nonetheless, the lessons are two-fold. First of all, when states start threatening direct economic sanctions, they may get to feel like great powers, but they are likely to fail in their goals. The second is that, had Beijing not succumbed to the temptations of geopolitical grandiosity, China might well have successfully embedded its technology – and perhaps its spyholes and back doors – in Britain's whole telecoms system.

BUYING A VOICE

Not everyone has such a weight in the global economy, though. Much cheaper, and if done properly much more cost-effective, is the bespoke influence operation. Money can be weaponised to buy a voice or to swing a vote, to muzzle a newspaper or to hype a project. Sometimes, this is through out-and-out corruption. We may like to think that this is less of an issue in most of Europe and North America, and in the main the old-fashioned handover of surreptitious envelopes of banknotes is a thing of the past. Large amounts of cash are hard to use in today's tap-to-pay economy, and unexplained wealth can be noticeable (and what's the point of taking bribes if you can't enjoy them?). That certainly does not mean that corruption is a thing of the past, though.

Surveys such as Transparency International's Corruption Perceptions Index – which identifies a spectrum of venality, with impoverished nations like Afghanistan and South Sudan at the bottom (most corrupt) and stable and prosperous Denmark and New Zealand at the top (least) – encourage the comforting delusion that development and honesty go hand in hand. Yet who does much of the bribery in the poorer countries? And where does most of that money end up? Italian supercars, French yachts, London penthouses, Scandinavian money laundries, shell corporations in Delaware and bank accounts in Liechtenstein. Corrupt is in many ways a racket that transfers assets from the poorer Global South to the richer North, but that's a whole other book.

What it does mean is that we cannot assume that this is a battle already won, or an easy one. There has been some progress – all too limited – with measures such as the US's Foreign Corruption Practices Act, the UK's Bribery Act and the FINCEN anti-money-laundering network. But corruption adapts, and is now often indirect. A non-executive directorship that pays well but demands little; an all-expenses paid 'fact-finding trip' to somewhere warm and comfortable; the loan of a holiday home; contributions for a re-election campaign. Although most democracies do have systems in place to monitor these kinds of influence-buying with greater or lesser success, patronage is as old as politics.

Nor is this necessarily a covert process. When the Nord Stream AG company was being set up to build the controversial Russian gas pipeline of the same name, majority shareholder Gazprom – which is in turn majority-owned by the Russian state – knew it faced some tough fights ahead. After all, the pipeline was not just an economic but a political venture. So to chair its board, it hired Gerhard Schröder, the former German Chancellor, for €250,000 a year, or almost three times his pension. Schröder has been an outspoken and effective lobbyist, as his job would require, and this is entirely above board.

Nonetheless, we need to recognise what former Estonian president Toomas Ilves has termed 'Schröderizatsia' – a word that has now entered German as 'Schröderisierung' and English as 'Schroederization', and which is used by political analysts and human rights activists to refer to the individual-by-individual corruption of another country's politics in a wholly legal (if ethically problematic) way. It is a leitmotif of the modern world. And if all else fails, you can rent what you cannot buy: lobbyists, PR specialists and 'reputation management' professionals of every stripe are there to help you get your message out and influence policy, for a fee. Examples such as Saudi Arabia's response to the Khashoggi murder have already been mentioned, but this is a huge global industry (worth $3.5 billion a year in the US alone), and pretty much everyone can join in. The overwhelming majority is corporate lobbying, but in an age when many companies are state-owned, state-influenced or just looking for a state's approval, the distinction may be moot.

Huawei's holding company, for example, is 1 per cent owned by Ren Zhengfei and 99 per cent by its workers – except that the workers themselves don't hold the shares, but a trade union committee which, in turn, pays its dues to the Shenzhen branch of the All-China Federation of Trade Unions, and this, of course, is controlled by the Chinese Communist Party. So when it lobbies, is it a private company or a state agency? Technically the former, but arguably in practice the latter. Likewise, until sold to Elbit Systems in 2018, Israel Military Industries was a wholly state-owned arms manufacturer. When it lobbied hard for sales to Turkey in the 2000s, at the very time that Tel Aviv was making its own overtures to Ankara, was this business driving politics or politics driving politics? The truth is that it is often hard to tell them apart.

Whether from crude corruption, jobs-for-the-boys patronage and favour-trading or professional lobbying, democracies and autocracies alike are vulnerable to this kind of influence from governments and their clients, pawns and proxies in the private sector. Why try and buy a country, when you may only need to buy a presidential adviser here or an influential parliamentarian there?

AGENTS OF INFLUENCE, AGENTS OF AFFLUENCE

Of course, it's better still if you don't have to tell them what to do. Never mind Machiavelli, perhaps today's would-be persuaders ought to listen to Winnie-the-Pooh. When asked what he likes best, A.A. Milne's amiably greedy bear pauses. 'Because although Eating Honey was a very good thing to do, there was a moment just before you began to eat it which was better than when you were, but he didn't know what it was called.' Money, like honey, is a treat to be savoured, but often it is its prospect that works best of all. Or, to put it another way, the thought of losing it may have an even greater impact than its actual loss.

Maybe the world has become too complex, too knowing for outright imperialism, whether by gun or by chequebook. Yet that hardly means that money does not buy power – arguably quite the opposite. Instead, the plausible goal has to be not rule, but domestication. When nations try and impose their will bluntly, through such instruments as sanctions, they typically fail. Instead, the subtler weaponisation of economic power is through conditioning the target towards useful habits, something the Russians

93

call 'reflexive control'. Sometimes this means carefully metred doses of negative reinforcement: maybe sanctions, or assets and industries can be targeted for cyberattacks, as discussed in Chapter 6, or raided and frozen through legal challenges, the topic of Chapter 8. This is ugly and obvious, though, and – as discussed already – is often of questionable value. It can easily backfire, stiffening backbones against foreign pressure.

Far better, though, are positive reinforcements that go with the grain of local politics and individual and factional self-interest. When Moscow supports populist parties and politicians in Europe, for example, it is not to change their views so much as because they already have views it considers useful. The leftist Five Star Movement and right-wing Lega Nord in Italy, the Alternative for Germany (AfD) anti-migration party and a host of other radical forces have been backed overtly by Russian state media and covertly by trolls and disinformation outlets not as part of any agreed quid pro quo, but simply because Moscow feels its interests would be served by their successes. More direct connections are less common, but also not unknown. In 2014, French nationalist Marine Le Pen's Front National party received a loan worth €9.4 million ($12.2 million) from a shady little Russian bank connected to the government after she had endorsed the annexation of Crimea. A hacked text from a Kremlin official saying 'she has not betrayed our expectations' later came to light.

But it is the prospect of personal and corporate gain that tends to be even more significant. The true force of China's $11 trillion economy is like gravity, warping orbits and raising tides without being visible to the naked eye. The political will to hold China to account for domestic human rights abuses and foreign aggression is constantly being undermined by a concern not to jeopardise investment and lose markets. Germany's debate about Huawei, for example, was influenced by a motor industry concerned it might be caught in any backlash, given that one in three German cars is sold in China. It is hardly alone. In 2008, when it was announced that the then French president Nicolas Sarkozy would be meeting the Dalai Lama, the spiritual leader in exile of Chinese-occupied Tibet, Beijing cancelled a series of trade visits and an order for 150 Airbus passenger jets was shelved. French industrialists, including car manufacturers and supermarket giants, frantically lobbied Paris, and the government duly issued a formal recognition that Tibet was part of China. The deals were back on, and state newspaper the *China Daily* gloated that 'France goes back on China's shopping list'. More recently, US businesses dependent on cheap industrial production in China complained loud and long about Donald Trump's escalating tariff war with Beijing. For years, the Chinese Communist Party leadership has had industries lobbying for its cause without it having to lift a finger or pay a single dollar or euro.

You don't need to be China to find you have more friends than you expected when the goose that lays the golden eggs comes under threat. Britain's position on EU sanctions discussions over Russia in 2014 were the subject of significant behind-the-scenes pressure from financial institutions and law firms that had got fat on Russian oligarch money flowing into the City of London. There is no evidence Moscow pressured them to do this: their self-interest drove them to campaign to dilute the penalties Russia had to pay for invading Ukraine.

Most striking is the political calculation behind Saudi Arabia's arms procurement policies. The kingdom spends with the profligate enthusiasm of an oligarch's mistress. Defence spending accounts for something like 10 per cent of its GDP – more than double Russia's share and five times the notional NATO baseline – and in 2020, 18 per cent of the national budget. At some $48.5 billion, this places it fifth in the world's league table of absolute military spending. Given that, with the exception of a minor part in the Gulf War, Saudi Arabia's sole recent military adventure has been its support for the government of Yemen in a continuing civil war, this seems excessive. But what Riyadh is really buying is influence. When it announces some new shopping binge, potential sellers scramble to win the deal. Defence industrialists become lobbyists at home, urging their national governments to overlook Saudi human rights abuses, to woo the kingdom. This explains why the Saudis have not only more aircraft, vehicles and other systems than they can use and maintain, but such a mix: US and European fighters, French, American and British ships, even a Chinese long-range missile. Perhaps it is significant that as concerns within the US about Riyadh's policies have increased since 2010, so too has the share of Saudi arms spending going to US companies. According to the 'Trends in International Arms Transfers' report published in 2019 by the Stockholm International Peace Research Institute (SIPRI), 70 per cent of its arsenal is now made in America.

Democratic societies and open liberal economies are much more vulnerable to this informal economic imperialism, and it is often scarcely visible when it is happening – and once accomplished, the victims police themselves. It is not states as such that are directly attacked so much as their elites. Industries, politicians and influencers can all be conscripted, co-opted, conditioned and compelled, sometimes without their even realising it. Newspapers accustomed to being paid to run lucrative infomercial inserts extolling the virtue of Chinese modernisation or

Saudi reform may opt to self-censor rather than lose them, just as universities hooked on foreign grants or students may quietly modify their policies to suit, even while loudly proclaiming (and technically still retaining) their independence. We are free – free to suborn ourselves.

In and of themselves, each of these effects may be relatively minor, sometimes even farcical. However, their real importance is two-fold. First, they accumulate, slowly building habits of deference and cooperation. Secondly, and perhaps most importantly, they combine with other instruments of modern conflict. It is far easier to shape the narratives that drive politics and policy if another country's media is already tamed, its experts compromised and its politicians bought and paid for (or at least rented from time to time). With not just money but also an already-favourable local establishment consensus, shaping laws and influencing policy becomes rather more possible. In other words, money is not just a weapon in its own right, it also makes all the other weapons that will be discussed in the following chapters that much more powerful. In this war, gold absolutely buys you good soldiers.

DEFENDING OR ENDURING?

So what can we do about it, in this age of what Henry Farrell and Abraham Newman call 'weaponised interdependence'? We all need to trade, to invest, to travel and to connect, so the answer cannot be autarky, an attempt to create hermetically sealed economies. The use of economic warfare and positive and negative influence is likely only to increase. The liberal credo that all trade is good and that nations which trade do not war is increasingly unsustainable, as these are no longer binary alternatives. As of writing, Indian and Chinese troops are sporadically clashing in a Himalayan border dispute that has seen soldiers clubbed to death and thrown off mountainsides. Yet bilateral trade between them is still worth over $100 billion. Unless one can see treaties that do for economic conflict what once they did for armed struggle and nuclear weapons – which may happen, some day – then nations too will have to decide what costs they are willing to endure to protect themselves, or even to use their economic muscle aggressively.

Nor is it always clear who is what. The Nord Stream 2 pipeline will take Russian gas to Germany across the Baltic seafloor. Germany regards this as a matter of economic security, ensuring a supply of lower-priced natural gas; Russia wants to sell the gas; America opposes it, claiming that it actually undermines European energy security by keeping it hooked on cheap Russian supplies; and cynics suggest the US just wants to sell more of its more expensive liquified natural gas (LNG). Washington is threatening sanctions against companies involved in the project, which at the time of writing is still under construction, albeit slowly. The truth of the matter is that everyone is self-interested (and to Germany, the US's heavy-handed approach itself came to be seen as a political security challenge), and everyone seeks to use whichever levers it has at its disposal.

In what will become a credo reinforced throughout this book, the three key answers are resilience; awareness and political will; and public vigilance. Resilience is obviously in part a matter of minimising risks. Where countries are most vulnerable, it is because they are over-dependent, whether on single sources of investment, energy or raw materials, or particular import or export markets. Some of this is hard to get around, but wherever possible, it needs to be a priority to diversify in every aspect. Ukraine's dependence on Russian gas (and the extra revenues from gas crossing its territory to Europe) meant it was vulnerable to periodic cuts and restrictions in supply – usually in the middle of winter. Nowadays, even if Moscow could afford to close the pipelines, Ukraine has more options, including American LNG. India has likewise been working to wean itself off Iranian oil since the imposition of sanctions.

Resilience is also a question of conviction: the capacity to accept economic costs as an acceptable price for political independence. This demands awareness and political will, two faces of the same coin. The challenges need to be discussed, analysed, game-planned and wargamed with the same vigour and candour as conventional military ones. Resilience needs to be not only worked into a country's economic strategies, but also required of its corporate national champions. For companies, this means a whole new level of political risk analysis and hedging dependence on specific markets and supplies. This will not come without a cost, and although sometimes public spiritedness and patriotism (or, less uplifting, the fear of negative publicity) may be an adequate spur, it more likely needs to be enforced and maintained by law, as well as supported by the state.

Governments also need to do much more to defend themselves and their societies from overt corruption and indirect influence. There is a general consensus on what this requires: proper transparency in political funding and lobbying, identification of the ultimate beneficial owner of organisations involved in such activity (so that they cannot hide behind shell companies and trusts), independent courts and well-drafted laws, rigorous enforcement of income declarations for officials and corporate governance in the private sector and a free and investigative media. The depressing truth is that these often break down in practice. Political parties don't want to give up the contributions on which they come to rely; industries that have grown to facilitate these questionable flows of money are reluctant to change; lobbyists and their clients are happy with the status quo.

All this will take political commitment, then, something which may be difficult to mobilise and maintain in the face of carrot-and-stick economic influence. As well as keeping a focus on the security dangers of becoming dependent upon and then moulded by another power, it can also be helpful to appreciate the potential advantages in resistance. Consider the example of Palau from the previous chapter, slammed by a Chinese boycott. In the short term, this brought economic pain, but its tourist boom was arguably unsustainable, driving up rents and food prices and encouraging quick and dirty developments with little thought of their impact on the local environment. Having endured the initial shock, Palau is now reorienting towards higher-value, lower-impact ecotourism and an arguably more sustainable and humane future path. In the future, Palau may feel it owes an ironic debt to Beijing for the unintended consequences of its attempt to bully its way to getting what it wanted. Likewise, China's blustering response to coronavirus may have saved the UK from a Huawei-dominated network.

Ultimately, though, governments can only be expected to keep up the pressure, and police their own donors, allies and friends, if they are forced to. That is the job of public vigilance. We get the governments we deserve, and if we as voters fail to require our political representatives to protect our national autonomy, then we have no one else to blame. Of course, though, if they cannot get what they want by (ab)using legitimate business and political structures, they may turn to illegitimate ones, and this is next for our consideration.

WANT TO KNOW MORE?

The best single survey of the world of corruption, lobbying and opaque global financing is Oliver Bullough's *Moneyland: Why Thieves and Crooks Now Rule the World and How to Take It Back* (Profile, 2018). *Kleptopia: How Dirty Money is Conquering the World* by Tom Burgis (William Collins, 2020) and *The Panama Papers: Breaking the Story of How the Rich and Powerful Hide Their Money* by Frederik and Bastian Obermayer (Oneworld, 2017) are also worth a read. *Thieves of State: Why Corruption Threatens Global Security* by Sarah Chayes (W.W. Norton, 2015) is a classic study of how graft is a security issue. It's easy to focus on the problem rather than solutions, but *Transitions to Good Governance: Creating Virtuous Circles of Anti-Corruption*, edited by Alina Mungiu-Pippidi and Michael Johnston (Edward Elgar, 2017), is about what to do.

CHAPTER 6

Crime

In September 2014, Estonian KAPO or security police officer Eston Kohver was heading out to speak with one of his inform-ants, a small-time smuggler called Maxim Gruzdev. The meeting would be in woods close to the village of Miikse, near the Russian border, but there was no particular reason to worry. He was working not on some high-risk, politically sensitive case but on the trail of some cigarette smugglers who were bringing counter-feit and untaxed tobacco across the border, avoiding Estonia's 30 per cent excise duty. It's the kind of low-level smuggling that happens all the time. Besides, he had his Taurus service pistol to hand, and a backup team was ready nearby. What could go wrong?

Suddenly, smoke grenades bloomed behind him, hiding him from the view of his colleagues, whose radios at the same time began to be jammed by military-grade transmitters. Kohver himself was dazed by a 'flash-bang' stun grenade and within seconds had been grabbed by heavily armed commandos from the elite Alpha anti-terrorist force of Russia's Federal Security Service (FSB), all balaclavas and body armour. They bundled him across the border. Within a day, he was in Moscow, accused of having intruded into its territory on an espionage mission – even though Russia's own border guards, obviously not let in on the plot, had signed a joint communique with their Estonian counterparts, confirming that the action had taken place on the other side of the frontier. It would be a year before Kohver would get home, swapped for Alexei Dressen, a KAPO officer who had been working for the Russians. But that was not why Kohver was kidnapped.

It emerged that the petty smugglers he was investigating had been suborned by the Russians. They were being allowed a free pass across the border in return for carrying out small-scale espionage missions. In addition, they were kicking a share of their profits back into European bank accounts that the Russians could use as a source of *chyornaya kassa* – 'black account' – money. These are funds with no apparent Kremlin fingerprints on them, which can then be used in pursuit of political operations in Europe.

Gruzdev actually turned out to be just one of a series of such smugglers-turned-assets: KAPO has identified at least five, often ethnic Russians with Estonian citizenship – the collapse of the USSR in 1991 left all kinds of communities mixed and stranded across the post-Soviet space – who had been recruited in this way. Typically, at some point they had been picked up or otherwise fallen foul of the FSB and offered the choice of a deal or prison – and a Russian prison, at that. No wonder they took the deal.

These are not big fish. Indeed, the Estonians call them *prügikala*, minnows or small fry. They can be used to gather basic intelligence. One, Pavel Romanov, started by giving the Russians information on the Estonian border guards before

being tasked with running down information on military installations and the kind of human-level intelligence no spy satellite
or communications intercept is likely to gather: gossip about
police and security officials, who was a drinker, who had money
problems, who had a wandering eye.

None of this was of critical importance, but the art of intelligence-gathering is at least as much about the patient collection
of these kinds of minutiae that may someday become valuable
– can that officer who gambles be recruited? – as the major operations and espionage coups. Each of these minnows was a minor
asset, a minor source of revenue, but also a minor investment
and a minor loss when they were caught. But together, they, and
all the other minnows that KAPO hasn't yet caught, complement Moscow's regular intelligence and influence operations.

Nor is this the only theatre for such activity. For example,
arguably the most effective of the so-called 'Illegals', the deep-
cover Russian agents uncovered in the US in 2010 (on whom
Moscow must have spent millions, and who probably never
reported much more than the best place to buy a latte in down-
town DC) was 'Christopher Metsos', whose real name was
probably Pavel Kapustin. When the rest of the network was
swept up by the FBI, 'Metsos' got as far as Cyprus, where his
trail disappeared. Several European security officers have told
me that they believe he was smuggled to Greece by professional
people-traffickers – experts, after all, in getting people across
borders – from where he could then be exfiltrated back to Russia.

THE GANGSTER-SPOOK NEXUS

There is nothing new in criminals being recruited as agents of
declared and undeclared wars. Hired assassins were a common

weapon in the struggles between Italian Renaissance city-states, principalities and families. As already noted, privateers – sanctioned pirates – were used from ancient times. In the Second World War, the US government and the Mafia made their own deals. First, the gangsters watched for Axis spies and saboteurs in the New York docks on behalf of the US Office of Naval Intelligence, later branching out to suppressing labour protests. In due course, they would provide local allies and intelligence to help the Allies seize Sicily in 1943, in return for being granted a free hand to re-establish themselves in southern Italy, regaining much of the ground lost to Fascist policing.

During the Cold War, the Mafia were commissioned to kill Cuban revolutionary leader Fidel Castro, and while one hand of Washington desperately fought the cocaine cartels of Latin America and their friends and facilitators, another used them against Soviet influence. A blind eye was turned to 'Contras' buying guns to fight the revolutionary regime in Nicaragua with cocaine profits. Panama's military dictator Manuel Noriega, a man who made millions by turning his country into a traffickers' paradise, was a close ally of the CIA until the brutal way 'Pineapple Face' ran his country and the increasing flagrancy of his corruption pushed the US into toppling him in 1989.

Not that the Americans were unique in turning to the dark side for convenient agents and allies. From the first, the Soviets had used criminals as instruments at home, from building up their secret police to controlling the Gulag labour camps. They were hardly likely to be any more fastidious about employing them abroad. They found a particular constituency in guerrillas, radicals, revolutionaries and terrorists. The German Baader-Meinhof Gang (they preferred the term Red Army Faction) was at one point even given sanctuary in Soviet-controlled Poland.

As for the Palestinians who for a while were hijacking aircraft on an almost industrial scale, Romanian defector Ion Mihai Pacepa claimed that General Alexander Sakharovsky, head of the KGB's foreign intelligence arm, boasted: 'airplane hijacking is my own invention'.

However, they were not above using non-ideological criminals, too. When Moscow allowed more Jews to emigrate to the US in the 1970s, for example, they used it as an opportunity to empty their prisons of Jewish career criminals. Most built new, legal lives for themselves, but some, like Evsei Agron, the gangster who made himself boss of New York's Russian and Jewish Brighton Beach neighbourhood – and whose favoured instrument was an electric cattle-prod – stuck to their thuggish ways. From Moscow's point of view, this dumped one of their problems onto their geopolitical rival, and some of those expelled gangsters might even become potential agents in the future. Meanwhile, Soviet allies and client states from Cuba to Bulgaria were implicated in drug- and gun-running, under the supervision of the KGB, to combine making mischief for the West with earning much-needed dollars.

NEW (UNDER)WORLD ORDER

In the shadows of the post-Cold War global underworld, criminality, from recruiting gangsters and manipulating flows of drugs, guns and migrants through to simple corruption, has become increasingly significant in the new geopolitical conflicts. Gangsters help pariah states break sanctions and raise funds. North Korea, for example, has so formalised this that Central Committee Bureau 39 of the Workers' Party of Korea, for all its long-winded title, is in effect the Hermit Kingdom's organised crime office. It traffics methamphetamines (brewed in government laboratories) and fake foreign banknotes (printed in the government mint) and smuggles out everything from coal to fake 'Made in China' textiles (all coming, of course, from government mines and factories). Often, it works with other parts of the state to raise funds: according to the EU, it was behind a scam whereby the Korea National Insurance Corporation was involved in international frauds that a defector said earned Pyongyang tens of millions of dollars every year. Much of the estimated $500 million to $1 billion it makes every year goes to supporting the lifestyle of Supreme Leader Kim Jong-un, but it has also bankrolled the country's nuclear programme and bought the advanced computers that North Korean hackers use to commit cybercrimes – and thus make more money – and harass opponents around the world.

North Korea is hardly the only country that has been able to bypass or minimise sanctions through criminality. Although it has mainly been warlords and insurgents who have funded themselves through 'conflict minerals' such as the $125 million a year's worth of 'blood diamonds' Sierra Leone's brutal Revolutionary United Front smuggled into international markets, it can also be states. In 2004, the Republic of the Congo was expelled from the UN's Kimberley Process, a scheme meant precisely to exclude 'blood diamonds', because the deeply corrupt Sassou Nguesso regime had managed to export one hundred times more diamonds than it officially produced. Clearly this was sanctions-busting, fronting diamonds mined across the borders in the Democratic Republic of Congo and Angola. Nonetheless, for a few years, it provided a lucrative additional source of revenue for a government that otherwise had few friends and a ruling circle with expensive tastes.

Iran is under sanctions, so its Revolutionary Guard Corps gets into the business of smuggling heroin (and taxing smuggling across Iran's borders by existing gangs) to raise funds for its modernisation and operations abroad. Its elite Quds Force moves Afghan heroin to Europe, for sale to local criminal networks, and the US government identified General Gholamreza Baghbani, one of the Revolutionary Guard's senior officers, as a 'specially designated narcotics trafficker'. Venezuela is under sanctions, and according to the US government, it has cut deals with drug traffickers, including the Colombian narco-terrorist movement FARC, allowing their cargoes and planes free movement across the country in return for a cut.

In the 1990s, though, the biggest fear was that criminals would acquire nuclear materials or even weapons from the ramshackle and under-controlled arsenals of the former Soviet Union. These held some 39,000 nuclear weapons and about 1.5 million kilograms of plutonium and highly enriched uranium. Might gangsters hold nations to ransom or sell warheads to rogue states looking to buy an oven-ready nuclear capability? It was not a wholly ridiculous fear. In 1993, for example, two down-on-their-luck Russian naval officers drove to the Sevmorput naval shipyard outside the northern port-city of Murmansk and bypassed the two bored soldiers standing guard at the gate by the simple expedient of squeezing through one of several holes in the security fence. They sawed their way through the old padlock on the door to the bunker containing fuel for nuclear submarines and stole three of the hundred uranium fuel rods they found there. As disgruntled military investigators later noted, 'even potatoes are guarded better'. The thieves were caught six months later when they confided in a colleague, hoping he could help them sell the uranium – they had not even thought about how to make money on the theft when they committed it.

These were not exactly emperors of crime, and this helps explain why the James Bondesque extremes of the worst-case scenarios never came to pass. After all, as an Israeli official probably not wholly unconnected with their sharp-toothed intelligence agency, Mossad, once told me: 'Gangsters want to enjoy their profits. They know that if they threatened the state of Israel, let alone sold terrorists a nuke, we would never rest, never let up, never let anything get in the way of retribution.'

There was something of an underworld market in nuclear materials, although typically more like the Murmansk case, a couple of chancers with a car boot stuffed with low-level radio-active material liberated from a factory making medical scanners or the like. They would more likely than not end up trying to sell their loot to undercover police officers. Indeed, a whole economy emerged around the entirely mythical 'red mercury'. Purportedly, this was a super-secret Soviet invention, the alchemical key to everything from atom bombs to the coatings for stealth aircraft. For a while, this generated a bizarrely self-sustaining cycle, as con men tried to convince potential buyers to pay $100,000, $200,000 or even, in one outlier of a case, $1.8 million for a kilo of what was often nothing more than some random red liquid, lightly irradiated to add verisimilitude. Meanwhile, terrorists (allegedly including Osama Bin Laden), rogue states and intelligence agencies running sting operations all tried to buy the material, encouraging yet more confidence tricksters into the game. By the 2000s, this make-believe market had pretty much played itself out, but there was still a bizarre re-emergence in Saudi Arabia in 2009. Rumours spread that Singer sewing machines had red mercury in their needles. Quite why this would be the case was never really explained, but none-theless the market price for these machines suddenly increased ten-fold. Seeing a lucrative new market emerge, gangs started breaking into tailors' shops and warehouses to steal them. How far the purchases, like the thefts, were essentially speculative forays, as people hoped the market would rise further, is uncer-tain, although there were the inevitable rumours of some force being keen to buy up the sewing machines, from a Kuwaiti multinational to even more shadowy players.

Instead, the real nuclear traders wear suits and lab coats. Pakistani nuclear physicist Dr Abdul Qadeer Khan was the man behind his own country's uranium enrichment industry, a crucial element in its nuclear weapons programme, passing on the secrets he had learned previously working at the European Uranium Enrichment Centrifuge Corporation. He also set up a string of front companies to buy the components that Pakistan could not build. He didn't stop there, though, and the so-called AQ Khan network has been linked with trafficking not bombs or isotopes but know-how: thanks to him, Iran and Libya were able to build their own enrichment centrifuges. Furthermore, Pakistan needed missile technology to deliver its bombs, and North Korea had missiles but wanted something more pyro-technic to fit on them – so through the 1990s, Khan brokered a steady trade of knowledge between the two, and sanctions-busting turned into a reciprocal exchange. In 2004, Khan's actions were officially deplored by Islamabad, and he was placed under house arrest, but a comfortable one, in his sprawling estate on the outskirts of the capital. Despite US pressure, in 2009 he was formally freed. Since then, he has been feted as a national hero, the Mohsin e-Pakistan, or saviour of Pakistan. Who says crime doesn't pay?

In other words, with an estimated annual turnover of over a trillion dollars and an interconnectedness spanning the globe, the underworld becomes a tempting and dangerous tool with which to challenge the international order. There is always a cost to doing so, in international reputation and even domestic security (since deals with criminals are prone to being renegotiated), but if the alternative is surrender, then these regimes will generally be very willing to pay it. Furthermore, the underworld is not only an essentially defensive asset, able to mitigate the impact of pressure from without; it can also be used as an all-too-offensive one, a weapon which is both deniable and also asymmetric, which even the smallest country can – if it is prepared to take the risk – use against a larger one.

'PATRIOTIC HACKERS' AND CYBERMERCS

Dark Basin is, or maybe was, a hacker-for-hire group. It reportedly created no fewer than 28,000 web pages looking like popular sites such as YouTube and Dropbox, to which phoney emails tried to direct hundreds of journalists, advocacy groups, politicians and companies. They were part of so-called 'spear phishing' attacks, which would try and fool the victims into typing in their passwords, which could then be used to access their private data and emails. The targets included environmental campaigners such as Greenpeace and the Union of Concerned Scientists, who had tangled with the oil industry, as well as critics of a German technology company that was under suspicion of accounting fraud. Some ended up being bombarded with emails daily, others had their private correspondence leaked on the net.

A report by Citizen Lab, an initiative of the University of Toronto's Munk School of Global Affairs and Public Policy,

111

expressed 'high confidence' that this bore the hallmarks of an Indian company called BellTroX InfoTech. An obscure technology consultancy, its office address turns out to be a room above a tea stall, but it nonetheless advertises itself as a cyber-intelligence provider with the punchy slogan 'You desire, we do!' What certain clients, their identities hidden by a thick veil of front organisations, non-disclosure agreements and legal firms, desired, it seems, was to inconvenience, intimidate and intrude into the privacy of their enemies, and someone 'did'.

This is part of a wider trend, the rise of organised cyber-mercenaries who can do everything from cracking into secure communications networks to harassing individuals, and who market their services to whomever wants them. At first, that tended to be criminals and the private sector. Want to steal 50,000 hotel rewards points from someone else's account? According to Dell's SecureWorks, the going rate is as low as $10. But for $10,000 a month, a British hacker known as Spdrman was hired by a senior figure at one Liberian telecoms company to target a rival, which he did with such enthusiastic overkill in 2016 that he crashed the entire Liberian internet.

Hackers will crop up throughout this book: as more and more of the world becomes e- and virtual, it may well be that at some time we will think that talking specifically about 'cyber-crime' is redundant, simply because so many offences will have migrated to the internet. Certainly, the internet is the best friend of hostile nation and greedy gangster alike. However, it is worth dwelling here for a while on the specific ways that states use the new capacities of the internet.

Sometimes they themselves carry out activities most usually associated with regular cybercriminals. North Korea's Reconnaissance General Bureau, for example, has been implicated in a number of online heists, such that in 2019 a UN Security Council report estimated that its hackers had stolen some $571 million in just twenty months of activity. The tally of crimes blamed on Pyongyang is impressive: the theft of $81 million from the Bangladeshi central bank's account at the Federal Reserve Bank of New York in 2016; $13.5 million from India's Cosmos Bank in 2018; $10 million from the Bank of Chile's ATM network. For a country hovering on the edges of starvation, such attacks are a valuable and viable way of raising funds – while thumbing one's nose at a hostile outside world.

At other times, the states recruit the hackers. As Russia's various and competing intelligence and security agencies came to appreciate the value of cyber-operations, the Foreign Intelligence Service (SVR) and military intelligence (GRU) took the conventional route, hiring smart young computer science graduates and building up their cyber-capacities. The Federal Security Service (FSB) – Vladimir Putin's old service and arguably both more cocky and less constrained by rules and traditions – thought it could take a short cut. It had long had close links with the hacker world. It would whip up 'patriotic hackers' when Moscow wanted massive attacks against targets such as Estonia in 2007 (because of a dispute over the removal of Russian memorials), Georgia in 2008 (during the brief Russo–Georgian War) and Ukraine from 2014 (in parallel with its military-political interference). Many were genuinely happy to help their state; others were essentially offered the choice of participation or incarceration.

The FSB then went further, offering certain hackers a job inside TsIB, its Centre for Information Security, again as an alternative to prison. This was an offer they couldn't refuse. It's no surprise, though, that many were not suddenly metamorphosed into loyal drones of the state by being given a military identity card and rank. What the FSB thought of as a cunning way to steal a march on their rivals and get a hacking capability off the shelf actually led to criminals gaining the opportunity to carry out their crimes with all the powers of the state, or to put some business in the way of their old mates. For example, Major Dmitry Dokuchayev, who as a hacker had gone by the name 'Forb', was accused by the FBI of engaging the three hackers who stole the data of half a million Yahoo users in 2014: he was after intelligence data, and the hackers could then sell the rest.

However, the temptation also to use this access for their own purposes seemed irresistible. Arguably, it was why they had become hackers in the first place. Embarrassingly enough, in late 2016, the FSB had to arrest Dokuchayev, along with TsIB's deputy head, Sergei Mikhailov. They were eventually convicted on treason charges, but were also reportedly involved in a series of criminal operations. Not least, they were connected with Anonymous International, a group of hackers known for leaking Russian government documents and embarrassing information about senior officials, sometimes for money, sometimes for deviltry, posting it on their blog, *Shaltai Boltai* ('Humpty Dumpty').

Of course, this is not only a Russian issue. Both Chinese and North Korean state hackers also apparently moonlight for personal gain. The hacking group known in the West as Advanced Persistent Threat (APT) 17 is run by the Jinan bureau of the Chinese Ministry of State Security, for example, but its tools and style of operation proved identical to those of the hackers of APT41, a team involved in private hacking and even selling its services for hire. Tellingly, members of APT41 and APT17 never seem to be operating at the same time, lending weight to the notion that they are one and the same: government operators using the advanced tools at their disposal for some after-hours enrichment.

Either way, the blurring of the boundaries between legal states and illegal networks, crime and statecraft, is most evident in the uncontrolled and rapidly changing realms of cyberspace. These are new opportunities, sometimes wholly new crimes. The irony is that the other particular opportunity for states to use gangsters as an instrument of hidden war is – if one excludes scrumping an apple from the Tree of Knowledge – the oldest crime of all: murder.

ASSASSINATION, INC.

Rojava in northern Syria is a region whose majority Kurdish population rose against the brutal regime of Bashar al-Assad, yet which was equally opposed to Islamic State jihadists and also the neighbouring Turkish government, which has for generations oppressed its own Kurds. Instead, they hoped amidst the chaos of the Syrian Civil War to be able to form their own independent, or at least autonomous, territory. The secretary-general of the Kurdish Future Syria party, Hevrin Khalaf, was driving with two others down the M4 highway in October 2019 when gunmen stopped the car and dragged her out of it. She was executed on the roadside, her bullet-riddled body filmed on a phone, destined for the internet.

This happened a few days after the Turkish military had launched its own offensive in northern Syria, determined to stamp hard on any prospect of a Syrian Kurdish state. The murder was clearly targeted, not a random act of violence. Her family, Future Syria and international human rights bodies all suspect it was carried out by Ahrar al-Sharqiya, an Islamist militia armed and bankrolled by Ankara. As Amnesty International put it, Turkey was 'outsourcing war crimes to armed groups'.

Sometimes, after all, states want to kill – indeed, feel they need to kill. They can use their own operatives, but this carries with it all kinds of risks, especially in the modern, supersaturated panopticon society in which every smartphone, every security camera, every computerised flight or hotel record can create a trail. When a fifteen-strong team from the Saudi General Intelligence Directorate lured dissident journalist Jamal Khashoggi to be murdered in their consulate in Istanbul, they had no idea they were being recorded, and it would become an international scandal. When two GRU officers tried to poison former spy Sergei Skripal in 2018, they had no idea that they would be identified so quickly or that this would trigger an international wave of expulsions of 153 Russian agents and diplomats from 27 countries.

Assassinations have become too difficult to conceal, too provocative to ignore. (And not everyone can rely on drones to kill those they would see dead, or get away with their use.) Instead, though, the state can turn to the professionals in murder when they want to reach out and touch someone. A string of Chechens who either fought against Moscow in their two failed wars of independence or provided the rebels with funds and support have been killed across Europe. Time and again the killers have turned out to be gangsters, hired for the job. The neo-Nazi car thieves from Moscow who travelled to Turkey in 2011 just to gun down three Chechens and then head home, for example. Or the wanted contract killer – whose criminal records had mysteriously been wiped – who walked up to a Chechen in Berlin in 2019 and shot him twice in the head.

Everyone may assume Moscow's hand ultimately pulled the trigger, but proving it is that much harder.

The Russians are especially willing and able to use gangsters as agents, but they are not alone, especially if we broaden the aperture from murder to include the associated application of violence and intimidation. When China was regaining control of Hong Kong in 1997, it specifically encouraged the Triad organised crime groups to stay, saying that 'patriotic Triads' had nothing to fear. But there clearly was a quid pro quo, and since 2014, protesters against Beijing have been assaulted by thuggish gangs of young men showing even less restraint than the police. Nor is this confined to Hong Kong: Taiwan's China Unification Promotion Party was founded by a former leader of the United Bamboo triad, who spent much time on the mainland. It regularly stages violent protests, not least to destabilise the country and undermine its institutions and democratic viability.

EXPEDITIONARY WARFARE, *GODFATHER*-STYLE

Do these kinds of operations really matter in the grand scheme of things? Although criminals, like the hacker who crashed Liberia, may play a role in the kind of weaponised anarchy discussed in Chapter 11, in the main they are not going to bring down a country or force a 180-degree change in policy, although they can undermine sanctions. The real impacts of the weaponisation of crime are subtler. They are a substantial force multiplier for other aggressive means of coercion and suasion. They can be – and are – used to raise 'black account' funds to support political subversion. They are able to silence whistle-blowers and annoying critics. They hack the compromising information your spies can exploit. In the final analysis, as yesterday's Americans showed in Sicily and today's Russians have demonstrated in Ukraine, hostile states can even use organised crime to pave the way for more conventional military operations.

Secondly, they eat away at the political and economic resources of a target state. If smugglers are crossing your borders with impunity, if hackers seem to be able to make sport of your critical systems without trouble, if gangs are brawling and killing in your streets without fear, then how credible does your state appear, and how likely is it that people will start looking for alternative, radical solutions to their worries? Tough-on-crime rhetoric has eased the rise of corrupt authoritarian populists from Rodrigo Duterte in the Philippines (who vowed 'to litter Manila Bay with the bodies of criminals') to Jair Bolsonaro in Brazil (who affirmed that 'a policeman who doesn't kill isn't a policeman'), many of whom adopt what has been called a 'pay to play' approach, whereby foreign countries and companies can flout local laws and shape policy, if the right people prosper. At other times, the need to fight crime may even leave a country open to leverage. For example, south-eastern Myanmar's Karen region, long troubled by vicious conflict between separatists and government forces, witnessed the emergence of all kinds of criminal businesses, such as illegal casinos and industrial zones, largely connected to Triads forced out of Cambodia. Such has been the scale of the problem that Myanmar had to turn to China for assistance in dealing with it, further tightening its dependence on its northern neighbour.

More generally, crime costs. Britain's National Crime Agency in 2019 estimated that serious and organised crime cost the country at least £37 billion a year: close to the same size as the total UK defence budget. If you are having to divert resources to customs patrols and drug treatment centres, to fraud restitution programmes and police restructuring, then that money cannot be spent on the military, or foreign aid, or other instruments of power projection. Speaking of power projection, states can use the underworld to bypass and undermine sanctions and other instruments often used to try and curb aggressive or transgressive regimes.

Furthermore, the economic penetration described in the previous chapters is often carried out with or in collaboration with criminals. Operation Sidewinder was a joint Royal Canadian Mounted Police and Canadian Security & Intelligence Service investigation looking at the strategic purchase of businesses and property by Chinese Triads linked to Beijing's intelligence agencies. On that basis, it concluded that 'China remains one of the greatest ongoing threats to Canada's national security and Canadian industry'. That may not come as a shock; what perhaps is more alarming is that the report dates back to 1997, and that it was suppressed, appearing later in drastically watered-down format. Ottawa seemed even then reluctant to admit the presence of a 'gangster-spook nexus' and to alienate Beijing. Yet the same pattern has emerged time and again since, from Australia to Zimbabwe. The Russians may gather intelligence using 'minnows', but China's spies and hidden influencers ride their country's sharks, instead.

POLICING IS SECURING

The relationship of crime and state has always been a complex one. This is not simply about a few gangsters being used for muscle or intelligence. Just as the state-making processes of the late medieval and Renaissance eras echoed, as Charles Tilly observed, the tactics of organised crime, so too today the boundaries between states and gangs have become more permeable than we might want to admit. The pirates of Somalia's Puntland regime reinvented themselves as pirate-hunters when the deal with the international community was right, and in the process formed their own de facto state. It may not yet have official recognition, but it has its own navy, flag, TV channel and airport. The breakaway slice of Moldova calling itself the Transnistrian Moldavian Republic was likewise created in the 1990s as a joint venture between local gangsters and Russian imperialists. The ongoing war in south-eastern Ukraine owes part of its longevity to the way that the 'People's Republics' are run by and in the interests of warlords and smugglers, who profess loyalty to Moscow while often making their money at even its expense.

If the boundaries between crime and statecraft have become more blurred than ever, then we need to treat the former as seriously as the latter. The underworld is, after all, often defined by the tolerances of the 'upperworld'. After 9/11, for example, the need to combat al-Qaeda led to a very successful US-led campaign against terrorist financing. The networks moving and laundering 'dark money' came to realise that it was dangerous and expensive to handle jihadist funds, and either refused or jacked up their prices to ruinous levels. (Al-Qaeda was sometimes forced to turn to couriers carrying suitcases of diamonds and banknotes – many of whom took the opportunity to abscond into well-funded new lives.) However, since then we have failed to learn the wider lessons. We did not crack down on the channels and brokers who move and launder money around the world for criminals, kleptocrats, tax-evading billionaires and corporations alike; we simply persuaded them not to deal with one very specific client.

Likewise, for all that states pay lip-service to the way that crime is also a security issue, in the main this does not play out in practice. This is hardly surprising: police and security officers work in different ways and have different goals. The police seek to make the streets safe and rely on cases won with evidence presented in open court. The spooks may well be more interested in disrupting activities, 'turning' individuals, feeding false information and otherwise prioritising state over public security.

This is as it should be. If security agencies always had to rely on sources they could stand up in court, they would be hamstrung; if we let cops get away with not doing so, then we are on the way to becoming a police state. However, there needs to be a serious and sustained focus on those crimes and criminals which appear to be facilitating malign foreign interference. Resources, after all, are a frequent constraint on policing. Forces operating with limited budgets and often labouring under unrealistic social and political expectations will prioritise operations on the streets and cases likely to lead to a quick and successful conviction. Serious organised crime, kleptocratic money movers, gangs linked with intelligence agencies – all of these tend to be hard targets, steeped in considerable operational security and able to hire the best lawyers and lobbyists to fight their corner.

To deal with them, law enforcers may need new or better laws – especially when it comes to 'dark money' – but generally require both the resources to do the job and also the space to do it. Such investigations are often lengthy, expensive and hard to bring to a successful conviction. The police and prosecutors need to be allowed to fail – within reason – lest a blunt obsession with conviction rate metrics force them to avoid such tricky cases.

Furthermore, nations must be willing to follow through with their pious pledges to fight corruption across the globe, even when it becomes economically disadvantageous or politically sensitive. In the Balkans, for example, the European Union preaches transparency, but for a long time has been happy to tolerate, even encourage, so-called 'stabilocrat' leaders, who talk the right democratic talk while running semi-authoritarian regimes and kleptocratic schemes that enrich themselves and their backers. Short-term political expediency time and again trumps a genuine willingness in Brussels to devote will and resources to making good on its fine words. This means promoting true independent media and imposing penalties on regimes which suppress them. It means serious and sustained aid for local police, judiciary and oversight bodies. It means direct pressure on the kleptocrats and their freedom to bank, spend, holiday and invest abroad. Above all, it means a willingness to accept that in the short term, the kleptocrats will not be happy. They may well turn to other patrons, states for which corruption is an asset, not a problem. So be it. There has to be the confidence that in the long term they – or more likely their political successors – will want to come in from the cold, as well as an understanding that this will not be a quick or easy struggle.

While crime is an increasingly useful instrument of hostile states, criminals are pragmatic. Measures to raise the risks and costs of such collaboration are the best responses and have already – as al-Qaeda discovered – been shown to work. We will, alas, never eliminate criminality, but we can at least define the parameters of 'acceptable gangsterism'.

WANT TO KNOW MORE?

Letizia Paoli's edited collection, *The Oxford Handbook of Organized Crime* (OUP, 2014), is not cheap but does cover the ground, as does Misha Glenny's intensely readable *McMafia: Seriously Organised Crime* (Vintage, 2017). There are many excellent books on criminality and its relationship to the state, with James Cockayne's *Hidden Power: The Strategic Logic of Organised Crime* (Hurst, 2016) one of the best and most recent. For a fascinating anthropological perspective, see *Global Outlaws* by Carolyn Nordstrom (University of California Press, 2007). On AQ Khan, Gordon Corera's *Shopping for Bombs* (Hurst, 2006) is a good read, and I look more at Moscow's use of criminals abroad in my *The Vory* (Yale UP, 2018).

PART III

War is All Around Us

CHAPTER 7

Life

The four heavily laden trucks rolled onto the bridge, a crowd of protesters behind and around them. At the far end, several hundred police and security troops hefted truncheons and grenade launchers. They would not let the trucks past. The protesters started chanting and jeering, pushing against the serried plastic riot shields, trying to shoulder their way through the phalanx. Stones started to fly, and teargas shells and rubber baton rounds came in response. A confrontation became a brawl, and suddenly one of the trucks was on fire, then a second. The protesters would claim the government forces deliberately burned them, but camera footage later revealed they were hit by a Molotov cocktail inaccurately thrown by one of the protesters. This was the Francisco de Paula Santander bridge between Colombia and Venezuela, on 23 February 2019. And what was inside these trucks that the security forces were so eager to keep out? Anti-government propaganda? Guns? No, food and medicines, for a country suffering from shortages and hyperinflation.

Aid is rarely the purest fruit of altruism. Recently re-elected Venezuelan president Nicolás Maduro had presided over an era of maladministration, corruption and unwise dependence on oil exports. What as recently as 2001 had been South America's richest country was falling into chaos. Inflation had gone stratospheric in the course of a single year, rising from 9 per cent at the start of 2018 to 10 million per cent. One in ten Venezuelans, from impoverished farmers to bright young technocrats, had fled the country. Organised crime, often working hand in hand with corrupt officials, was running riot: the murder rate was about double Colombia's, even at the height of Bogotá's undeclared civil war against narco-terrorists.

Long irked by the inflammatory rhetoric and adventurist leftist policies of Maduro and his patron and predecessor, Hugo Chávez, the US swung its support behind opposition leader Juan Guaidó. He had stood in the presidential elections as the candidate of the social democratic Popular Will party and – rightly – decried the vote as rigged. In January 2019, a month before the protests, he had declared that he was assuming power as acting president in his capacity as chair of the National Assembly. Constitutionally this may have been legal, but practically it was a non-starter. Despite his claims that the majority of the security forces would back him, and quick recognition from the US, Canada and many Latin American and European nations, Guaidó was unable to topple Maduro and was barred from leaving the country.

Later, there would be an abortive and rather farcical military incursion in May 2020, when two American mercenaries and sixty Venezuelan rebels launched a madcap bid to seize the airport, capture Maduro and bring down the whole regime. Unsurprisingly, they were soon rounded up by government forces. Although former national security adviser John Bolton claimed that Donald Trump said it would be 'cool' to invade Venezuela, in practice Washington was well aware of the risks in direct confrontation with a regime fielding over 120,000 soldiers and paramilitaries, and with the capacity to use the defence of the nation against 'yankees' as a potential tool to mobilise public legitimacy.

Instead, they looked to subvert it. The humanitarian situation was undeniably dire. Guaidó, presumably motivated by genuine compassion as well as political calculation, made particular play of the need to address the immediate needs of ordinary Venezuelans. He appealed for aid. Likewise, although not solely driven by statecraft, many countries that responded – including the US, where it was the hawkish Bolton, not aid officials, who took the lead – saw this also as a way of bolstering Guaidó and highlighting the regime's failures. In response, Maduro determinedly chopped off his own nose to spite his face, defiantly asserting that 'they want to treat us like beggars . . . There is no humanitarian crisis here'. Implausibly, he went on to claim that 'Venezuela is not a country of famine. It has very high levels of nutrients and access to food', even while researchers were finding that 80 per cent of the population was suffering from food insecurity. Hence the tragically ridiculous scenes at the Francisco de Paula Santander bridge, also played out at other border crossings, and even at sea, where a ship from Puerto Rico tried to deliver aid, only to be turned back by the Venezuelan navy under threat of being fired on.

A tragedy for the ordinary Venezuelans for whom the aid was intended, but a cynical win-win for Maduro's enemies. Had the aid gone through, it would have humiliated him. Conversely, the grotesque spectacle of paramilitaries forcibly turning the convoys away became a powerful symbol delegitimising the regime both at home and abroad. Although both China and Russia dutifully supported Maduro, even Moscow was clearly embarrassed by the situation.

WAR ON THE PEOPLE

War is hell, and its ways are often hellish. Starving out an enemy has been a commonplace of conflicts throughout history. Even worse, deliberately spreading disease was a vicious tactic used by combatants across the world, from the plague victims' corpses the Mongols catapulted into besieged cities in the thirteenth century to the smallpox-ridden blankets handed to Native Americans at Fort Pitt in the eighteenth. In the Renaissance, where close-clustered cities and regular trade made such tactics suicidal (germs, after all, respect no borders), instead the answer was to sack cities for plunder or, more indirectly, target a rival's agrarian base.

After all, cities grew precisely because increasing crop yields permitted the rise of populations working in commerce and industry, not on the land. People, in short, who relied on other people for their food. When English mercenary commander Sir John Hawkwood launched his Great Raid on Tuscany in the summer of 1375, he saw that threatening agrarian collapse was a powerful weapon against cities dependent on their rural hinterlands. This, not direct assault, gave him a way of holding cities to ransom. Pisa's resistance led him to begin kidnapping peasants and above all seizing livestock. Pisa capitulated, paying him 30,500 florins – equivalent to more than three times the initial capitalisation of the Medici Bank – to leave them be. Such raids became a regular feature of Renaissance war, striking not at the head, but at the stomach.

This was usually in the context of military operations, though. Today, in an age when biological weapons of mass destruction are rightly banned and shunned, the spread of hunger and disease has been replaced by the selective control of their remedies. Aid, water, medicines: all these humanitarian blessings have – not always, but arguably increasingly – been weaponised to bring enemies to their knees and regimes into disrepute, just as migrants become weapons in undeclared political conflicts. As we approach an age in which even control over the weather (and thus crop yields) becomes practical, humanitarianism has become a potential tool of statecraft and, sometimes, covert warfare.

A LITTLE HELP FOR MY FRIENDS

The Marshall Plan, more formally the European Recovery Plan, was arguably the most impressive and successful aid project in history. Between 1948 and 1951, the US spent more than $12 billion (equivalent to something like $130 billion in 2020 terms) on rebuilding a Europe shattered by the Second World War. Of this, 5 per cent went to the CIA for a range of covert political influence operations, such as setting up anti-communist front organisations and bankrolling supportive newspapers. However, it is probably fair to say that the whole Marshall Plan was at once an act of supreme generosity and of cynical manipulation. After all, this was aid with strings, intended to rebuild European states as capitalist liberal democracies, which is why Stalin not only refused it for the USSR but also forbade the newly conquered Central European nations of what would become the Warsaw Pact from accepting this largesse. The effect was not simply a dramatic economic recovery but also a stabilisation of the politics of Western Europe, halting and reversing the rise of pro-communist sentiment and buttressing regimes which saw America as a vital ally, as well as trading partner.

Aid is often – some would say almost always – an implicitly political act. It reflects the values and assumptions of the donors (on the morality of spending money on foreigners, and on which causes and countries are more deserving) and is frequently leveraged for political gain at home and abroad. There is a reason why USAID food consignments are proudly labelled as such, in red, white and blue, to make sure there is no doubt that Uncle Sam is the generous provider. (And, indeed, why Japanese Yakuza gangsters made a big deal of providing relief supplies after a devastating earthquake in 1995 and tsunami in 2011: they wanted full credit for their good deed.) Besides, aid budgets are often protected and extended by appeals to national self-interest. Aid is portrayed as a means of preventing unwanted influxes of migrants (by supporting the economies of poorer countries and staving off hunger), of reducing terrorism (by shoring up failing states), of winning new markets (by developing local demand) or of fighting off hostile political influence.

Tellingly, when British prime minister Boris Johnson announced in 2020 that the Department for International Development (DfID), with its £14 billion aid budget, was being rolled into the Foreign Office, it was explicitly to 'maximise British influence'. In his view, 'for too long, frankly, UK overseas aid has been treated as some giant cashpoint in the sky that arrives without any reference to UK interests or to the values that the UK wishes to express or the priorities, diplomatic, political or commercial, of the Government'. As an example, he said that the UK gave 'as much aid to Zambia as we do to Ukraine, though the latter is vital for European security. We give ten times as much aid to Tanzania as we do to the six countries of the western Balkans, who are acutely vulnerable to Russian meddling.'

This was unusually frank, but reflected a crucial division between those who would see aid go to who needs it most and those who would see it go to where the donor state needs it most. Ukraine's GDP per capita is almost double Zambia's, after all, but it is also a strategic country facing Russian pressure. The truth of the matter is that the latter have generally dominated the process, not just in the UK but in most donor nations.

There are various indices that could be used to assess which are the poorest countries in the world, but by combining the bottom five from each, eleven countries emerge more or less as the consensus most destitute: Burundi, the Central African Republic, the Democratic Republic of the Congo, Eritrea, Liberia, Malawi, Niger, Somalia, South Sudan, Tajikistan and Uganda. In contrast, by its own account, the top five benefici-aries of UK aid are Bangladesh, Ethiopia, Nigeria, Pakistan and Syria. As for the US, the lucky winners are Afghanistan, Ethiopia, Iraq, Israel and Jordan. The top five for Germany – which in 2020 announced that countries which were 'reform-resistant' and prone to corruption and human rights abuses would lose priority status for aid – are China (which has a total GDP around four times Germany's and endemic corruption), Colombia, India, Indonesia and Syria. And so it continues, with a clear disconnect between aid flows and practical need. Aid has always been and likely will continue to be heavily contingent on state-craft: security, geopolitics and trade. However, with China increasingly blending its own evolving aid programme with Belt and Road Initiative investment, with the US under Donald Trump having championed a nakedly transactional approach to international engagement and with the post-ideological world being also an increasingly competitive one, this may well become ever more overt.

THE BARE NECESSITIES

States give, and states take away. Foreign aid, worth some $170 billion globally, can be used by donors as a carrot, given to nations friendly enough, interesting enough or scary enough to be worth helping. However, potential recipients also compete not just for a share of this aid but also to play donors against each other, auctioning off their loyalties or agendas to the highest bidder. When, in 1956, the US backed away from promises to fund Egypt's Aswan Dam, the Soviets jumped in to help, seeing a chance to win a strategically significant ally. Today, countries such as Pakistan adroitly navigate between the US and China, and when Washington suspended $1.3 billion in aid in 2018, Beijing offered loans and further investment in return. A 2006 study in the *Journal of Political Economy* by Ilyana Kuziemko and Eric Werker with the giveaway title 'How much is a seat on the Security Council worth?' even found that countries taking up revolving seats on the UN's governing body could and did expect to get more aid, implicitly in return for their votes: an extra $16 million a year on average from the US alone, fully $45 million when key issues were in play.

Conversely, access to the most basic resources can be denied, controlled and restricted, made hostage to geopolitical interests. Consider one of the most fundamental human needs: water. Especially as climate change depletes some existing supplies and makes agriculture in warmer regions more precarious, this becomes all the more precious, and thus strategic. We may well see 'water wars' in the future, but in the meantime there is all the more scope to weaponise its access.

Thus, India's Kishanganga Dam not only powers a hydro-electric power station opened in 2018, it also diverts water from the Jhelum river, which flows on into the territory of its perennial enemy, Pakistan. This deprives Pakistan of about a third of the water normally flowing along the Jhelum. Islamabad has argued that this is a breach of a 1960 treaty, and managed to get an international ruling that India had substantially to lower the height of the dam. As of writing, though, Pakistan is claiming that India is still in breach – and meanwhile India is quite literally generating power at its expense.

Likewise, although Kyiv was unable to prevent Russia from seizing and annexing Crimea in 2014, the peninsula depends on water from deeper in Ukraine. By stopping the flow from the North Crimean Canal, Kyiv forced the Crimeans instead to rely on water from their own wells and reservoirs, which have steadily been drying up. Moscow has had to spend effort and money laying pipelines and drilling more wells, but ground-water levels are still falling sharply. For the foreseeable future, Crimea will have to cope with water shortages for people and agriculture alike. Moscow may well have to bankroll expensive desalination plants to allow seawater to be used. Is this war? A crime? Simply a refusal to subsidise Moscow's occupation of the peninsula? The nature of this modern style of strategic competition is precisely that it is hard to apply clear definitions, and easy to dispute them. At least – so far – no one in Crimea is starving, and the healthcare system is intact and working.

Water and food, after all, are inextricably linked. So too are water and health. In 2020, Turkish-backed militias in north-eastern Syria, almost certainly with Ankara's approval (maybe at its instigation) began using their control of the Alouk water station to cut supplies to Kurdish-held regions in which over a million people were confined. Their demand was that the Kurdish regions supply them with more electricity, but locally the belief was that this was part of a wider campaign to force them to accept Turkish dominion. What made this all the more of a problem is that it coincided with the coronavirus pandemic, when hand-washing, which requires clean water, was a crucial means of protection. A people in the midst of a civil war, who live a hand-to-mouth existence, are hardly going to be rich in antiviral hand sanitiser.

Denying access to healthcare is a depressingly common tactic in civil wars. Indeed, in Syria, the government has systematically shelled and bombed hospitals and clinics in rebel regions to punish them and induce them to surrender. When government forces launched an offensive on the Eastern Ghouta region in 2018, for example, its hospital capacity was reportedly halved in just four days of intensive bombardment, not least by the more advanced aircraft and skilled pilots of the Syrians' Russian allies. As a result, diseases such as polio and TB have re-emerged. The extension of this policy to those outside one's borders is every bit as immoral, and also represents another example of leveraging basic human necessities as a means of statecraft.

Along with food and water and healthcare, what else do people need? Heat and light, and energy is another a source of traction. When it could still afford to close the taps, and before its market control was undermined by plentiful supplies of liquefied natural gas – which can be moved by tanker and is thus more flexible than regular gas, which travels only by pipeline – Moscow several times used selective suspensions of gas supplies to bring pressure to bear on Ukraine. Having kept its energy prices artificially low to reward President Leonid Kuchma between 1994 and 2005 for his relatively friendly policy, Russia punished a new independence of spirit on Kyiv's part with coercive constrictions in supply. In 2006, it cut off supplies to both Ukraine and Georgia, and then again to Ukraine in 2009. In the latter case, all Russian gas to Ukraine was stopped for thirteen days in January – a hard, cold January – which also incidentally cut off supplies to south-eastern Europe. A new deal was struck, and Kyiv warned of the dangers of challenging Moscow; and while Russian gas corporation Gazprom lost an estimated $1.5 billion in revenue, the Kremlin presumably thought this was just the price of war.

WAR WITH THE PEOPLE, WAR WITH PEOPLE

Of course, pressure exerted one way can also go another. When Moscow stirred up risings in Ukraine's Donbas region, Kyiv called the people stuck there – disproportionately the old, who could not or would not uproot themselves and head westwards – victims of Russian aggression. In practice, though, it arguably treated them as collaborators, and stopped paying them their pensions unless they made it across the battlelines to collect them. According to the UN Human Rights Monitoring Mission in Ukraine, 700,000 lost access to their pensions as a result. One can argue the rights and wrongs of this move, but in the process, Kyiv lumbered Moscow, as the patron, protector and creator of the rebel Donbas and Lugansk 'People's Republics', with a humanitarian problem.

Innocent people are, and arguably always have been, weapons of war. Ethnic cleansing, displacing communities considered hostile or just alien, is a miserable corollary of conflict, from the mass internment and resettlement of 'dangerous peoples' such as the Muslim Uighurs of north-west China to outright massacres and expulsions, such as that practised by Serbs against Muslims and Croats in former Yugoslavia and by the Hutu against the Tutsi in Rwanda, both in the 1990s. However, migration, or even just its threat, is also a weapon of political war of particular relevance today.

Fewer than 500 kilometres of sea separate its shores from the Italian island of Lampedusa, and so Libya has become one of the particular gateways for migrants from Africa seeking to make their way into Europe, fed by a complex route system running from Senegal on the West African coast to Ethiopia and Somalia in the east. Dictator Muammar Gaddafi had in the early 2000s begun to work with the European Union to control the flow of migrants, for which his country was paid in cash and a return from the pariah status he had earned by past support for terrorism. In 2011, though, protests erupted and, eager to deter the EU from supporting the opposition, Gaddafi warned them to stop 'or I'll suspend cooperation on migration and Europe will be facing a human flood from North Africa'.

This became moot, as heavy-handed repression quickly turned protests into civil war, and by October 'the Colonel' would be dead, but his lesson endured. Today, Libya is still gripped by civil war, but one of the reasons southern European countries such as Italy and France are actively involved is precisely because they need to control the potential 'migration weapon' that a new Libyan leader could deploy.

This is not just a potential threat, after all: witness Syria and Turkey. The Syrian civil war, which began that same fateful year, 2011, and likewise shows no sign of ending, has led to massive levels of migration, some to other parts of the country, others across its borders. Millions of Syrians fled to neighbouring Turkey. In autumn 2019, Turkish forces and their local allies launched an offensive in northern Syria. Civilians died, and EU countries criticised the operation, threatening sanctions. In response, Turkish president Recep Tayyip Erdoğan warned that he would 'open the gates and send 3.6 million refugees your way', if they did not stop calling his attack 'an invasion'. An EU boycott of arms sales to Turkey went ahead – but instead of being mandatory, it was just voluntary. Likewise, the EU moderated its language: 'invasion' became 'unilateral military action'. Ankara continued to face public criticism, but the ever-pugnacious Erdoğan had deployed his 'weapon of mass migration' and secured at least a partial European climb-down.

CORONAVIRUS DIPLOMACY

Perhaps the most striking example of the way that health can be mobilised as an instrument of soft power, on the one hand, and coercion, on the other, is provided by the 2020 COVID-19 coronavirus pandemic. Moscow saw an opportunity to try and regain some lost ground in the West without actually having substantively to change its policies. Its 'From Russia with Love' campaign saw medics and equipment (sometimes of questionable value) sent to ally-of-sorts Serbia, friendly Italy and even the US.

The visuals of white-painted trucks rolling through NATO-member Italy and a massive military An-124 cargo plane landing at New York's John F. Kennedy International Airport certainly played well at home. Gains abroad were more limited. The latter initiative became, characteristically enough, a game of competitive trolling. Part of the Russian shipment to the US turned out to have been paid for by the Russian Direct Investment Fund, a state-owned sovereign wealth investment fund on a US sanctions list. In return, a batch of ventilators was later sent to Moscow under the auspices of USAID, the US Agency for International Development, which had been expelled from Russia in 2012. Point, counterpoint.

On the other hand, the contrast of Russia's high-profile initiative with what appeared to be indifference from EU partners certainly helped bolster growing Euroscepticism in Italy. A survey in April 2020 found 32 per cent of respondents describing Russia as a friend – and fully 45 per cent considering Germany an enemy, despite the fact that while Moscow donated just 300,000 protective masks, Paris and Berlin sent 2 million each. As PR, this was something of a success, but such operations tend to be short-lived in their effects. They are most effective when they work with the grain of public opinion – such as playing to Italy's Euroscepticism and traditional close relations with Russia – and above all as just one part of a long-term campaign to win soft power.

Beijing, by contrast, seemed unsure whether to be good cop or bad, and too quickly abandoned the former. It too launched a campaign of strategic and performative medical assistance, very much directed towards clients and those whom it wanted to woo, from Spain to the Gulf States, Kazakhstan to Colombia. (Again, it found itself competing with Taipei: Palau received nothing from China, but masks, thermometers and test kits from Taiwan.) Yet the Chinese government seems quickly to have given up on this approach. Instead, it demonstrated itself to be touchy to the point of hypersensitivity about its likely status as the original source of what Trump variously described as 'the Wuhan Virus' or, in a triumph of boorishness, 'Kung Flu'. When Australian prime minister Scott Morrison made the seemingly mild suggestion that there should be an international enquiry into COVID-19's origins, the Chinese state media pilloried him for 'panda bashing', one of the more bizarre invectives in Beijing's political lexicon. The Ministry of Culture and Tourism claimed there had been a 'significant increase' in 'racist attacks on Chinese and Asian people', and sanctions were imposed on a range of Australian imports. In a more sinister turn, an Australian who had been arrested fully seven years ago for smuggling drugs into China was suddenly sentenced to death, and a cyberattack presumed to originate in China hit a wide range of Australian government and business systems.

NO NEED FOR DESPAIR

Civilian lives have always been not just subjects of war but its objects and, sometimes, its weapons. We might like to think that being kind is its own reward, and in many ways it is. But sometimes being cruel seems easier and more effective. Gaddafi's and Erdoğan's threats, the way famine and disease have been deployed as weapons in Syria and Yemen, the burning trucks at the Venezuelan border, all this may seem to suggest that barbarism works.

It may win in one moment and in one theatre of operations, but in the process such tactics create a more dangerous environment for everyone. The answer is not just to decry this as a terrible thing, to make stirring speeches at the UN and to call out dictators whose reputations are in any case already stained beyond redemption. Rather, it is to remember that states are rarely engines of altruism, but sometimes need to look beyond the immediate tasks at hand. The answer is to come to terms with the extent to which the short-term gains of overt (ab)use of humanitarianism and aid are outweighed by the long-term dangers. Floods of migrants, mutating pandemics, insurgent and terrorist armies galvanised by anger, hunger and a sense of betrayal – these are all the costs of global inequality.

The need is not to end state aid, but nor to pretend that it is some apolitical global social security programme. Rather, it needs to be used smartly, and combined with effective measures to bring stability to foreign countries. It is easy to get lost in navel-gazing concerns about 'colonial attitudes' supposedly encoded within aid and development programmes, or to overlook how, despite valiant efforts to try and ensure that help gets where it is needed, too much actually ends up diverted by kleptocrats and simply winging its way back to the West, sitting in its banks or buying luxury cars and properties. As Pablo Yanguas writes in his splendidly provocative *Why We Lie About Aid*, 'whatever form aid takes, it will always have a profound effect on local actors, legitimising some and delegitimising others'.

There is truth in the cliché 'give a man a fish and you feed him for a day, teach a man to fish and you feed him for a lifetime'. But as the Somalis learned, there's little value in knowing how to fish if all your fish stocks have been raided. And as many other marginal communities around the world have discovered, if the fish you catch are then seized by warlords, kleptocrats or other exploiters, then you're still going hungry. Few Western countries really want to get seriously into the nation-building business, identifying it with the seemingly endless and fruitless US campaigns in Iraq and Afghanistan. Yet providing food and medicine is fish for a day, and even attempts to support local economies and grass-roots community activity is often no more than fish for a week, before they are crushed between uncaring market forces and local predators. If aid and development are to be weaponised, then that needs to be done not for the immediate benefit of the donor but the long-term life-chances of the recipients. And that must mean as much of a focus on creating capable, representative and honest government structures as digging wells and distributing vaccines.

Dambisa Moyo, a Zambian who went on to work at Goldman Sachs and the World Bank, asked 'what if, one by one, African countries each received a phone call, telling them that in exactly five years the aid taps would be shut off — permanently?' Her view was that this would be an energising wake-up call, forcing countries rapidly to pivot to increase trade and attractiveness to foreign investment. Of course, the risk is that some countries would spread their wings and fly, others crash and burn. And, of course, that China would buy all of the ones in between. Such provocative ideas likely work better on the page than in the field, but they do challenge us all to recognise that current aid strategies have too often been ineffective.

It is impossible to disconnect aid from its politics, whether it disrupts or reinforces existing social and political systems. The best we can do is to make sure it is a force not just for survival but for good – and that the geopolitical temptations to weaponise the basic necessities of life are resisted and punished.

WANT TO KNOW MORE?

Beyond *Why We Lie About Aid: Development and the Messy Politics of Change* (Zed, 2018) by Pablo Yanguas, other critical or imaginative takes on aid and development include Dambisa

Moyo's *Dead Aid* (Penguin, 2010) and Giles Bolton's *Aid and Other Dirty Business: How Good Intentions Have Failed the World's Poor* (Ebury, 2008). William Easterly's *The White Man's Burden: Why the West's Efforts to Aid the Rest Have Done So Much Ill and So Little Good* (OUP, 2006) may take a different angle, but is a classic of the field.

CHAPTER 8

Law

In 2012, *the MV Alaed, a Curaçao-flagged cargo ship, set out from the Russian port of Kaliningrad for Syria, carrying missiles and refurbished helicopter gunships for the beleaguered regime in Damascus. The European Union had imposed an embargo on the sale of weapons to Syria, as they were being used in the brutal suppression of the opposition. However, the ship was owned by a Russian company, Femco, and registered in a fairly autonomous island in the Dutch Antilles. It was not planning to dock at any European port on the way and, indeed, was taking a rather circuitous route with frequent changes in course, apparently to make it harder to track and also to avoid European territorial waters.*

This could have led to a major international row, but while the diplomats wrangled, the ship would have been sailing. In the films, this would have been a job for a single super-spy or a team of intrepid commandos, who would have sunk the ship or seized it and sailed it to a friendly port. To what weapon did the British government turn? Whom did they decide was more terrifying and formidable than a troop of Special Boat Service operators? The insurance industry.

The hub of the world's maritime insurance industry is Lloyd's of London, where policies are bought and sold, reinsured and underwritten. All eight of Femco's fleet were insured with Standard Club, a mutual insurance association run out of London, and the British government quietly had a word. All of a sudden, Femco's insurance was withdrawn, just as it was some 80 kilometres from the north coast of Scotland.

The insurers simply said that this was because Femco had 'broken internal rules', and nothing to do with any government action, although some sources later suggested that they had been threatened with legal consequences for aiding and abetting sanctions-breaking and potentially even war crimes. For the moment it meant that until the insurers could be reassured that the *Alaed* was not involved in 'improper or unlawful trade', it – and the rest of Femco's ships – were without cover. In theory, the ship could have continued, but above and beyond the risk of losing such an expensive asset if anything were to happen, there are all kinds of legal issues with a hull and a crew finding themselves uninsured. The ship turned around and returned to Russia. The *Alaed* would sally forth again with its lethal cargo in the future, but for the moment a crisis had been averted through the use of the law.

LAWFARE

The modern world, after all, is now shaped and bound by laws, which cut across national and political boundaries. The

International Criminal Court in The Hague seeks to provide some limits to wars and other conflicts. The United Nations Convention on the Law of the Sea rules and partitions the world's waters. International arbitration is vital for trade and investment across borders. The reach of law extends even beyond the bounds of the Earth: the 1967 Outer Space Treaty defines acceptable practice in orbit.

As with every aspect of human activity, and especially those which are transnational, the rise of international law – something that really only began with the Peace of Westphalia in 1648, but which has truly accelerated since the end of the Second World War – has also opened up new opportunities for strategic competition. A recent buzzword in the security realm is 'lawfare', the use and abuse of local and international law for national gain, and this is an arcane but increasingly powerful new battlefield. Of course, we see this in full form at the UN, where Beijing claims that the new islands it has built up from the seabed in the South China Sea allow it to extend its national waters, where Moscow claims that the Arctic is largely Russian based on disputed geophysical surveys, and where both Israel and the Palestinians seek to delegitimise the other. However, it is also a tactical tool.

Law can be mobilised as an instrument in a range of ways. The focus is usually on the malign: national libel laws used to suppress inconvenient news stories and even more inconvenient émigré dissidents. But refugees are also turned into living warheads thanks to asylum laws, or human shields used to prevent attacks by forces bound to observe the norms of modern warfare. Even the decision to issue passports can be tantamount to a land grab, as will be discussed later.

Lawfare even provides the European Union, which regards itself as an essentially peaceable bloc, with the opportunity to show some muscle. The world's largest single market likes to frame itself as a 'regulatory superpower', and it is able to use that to force other powers to conform to rules which, of course, are to its advantage. As the conduct of the Brexit negotiations demonstrated, such dry subjects as trade regulations are nonetheless still about power, and who gets to set terms to whom. Laws may be there for the common good, but the practice of law has always been confrontational, and so no wonder states turn to this arena, too.

WHO NEEDS ASSASSINS?

The Russian – not quite an oligarch, but still extremely rich: let's call him a minigarch – had not had a good day in court. He was locked in a business dispute over assets worth millions, stemming from allegations of contract violations in Russia, which were nonetheless being arbitrated in London. However much rich Russians may profess to love their country and respect President Putin, they nonetheless tend not to want to entrust their fortunes and futures to Russian courts. In any case, while the case was about money, the minigarch was sure it was about politics. As he transferred more and more of his assets into Europe, he was also trying to reinvent himself as a reform-minded, Westernised cosmopolitan. In the process, he had made some statements that seemed a little more critical of the Kremlin than might have been wise, and had bankrolled some causes that could be presented as affiliated with the opposition. He was sure this legal case was really driven by the Kremlin's desire to punish him, and that it was providing a business rival with documents to damage him. (I was, I should add, playing a very minor role in this case, supporting his legal team.) The documents were forged, of course, he was eager to assert, but he was having trouble convincing the court of this.

He sighed. 'Who needs assassins, when you can hire lawyers?'

Regardless of the merits of that particular case, it is clear that authoritarian regimes are increasingly seeking to exploit national and international law to suppress criticism and persecute political enemies. Well-funded legal actions, often backed with documents that may be fake but, having been provided by the state, look genuine in every respect, can replace or at least supplement more traditional methods such as murder and kidnap.

The UK and US have been especially attractive to 'libel tourism', the practice of shopping around for the most agreeable courts in which to make appeals. In 2004, for example, the author and scholar Rachel Ehrenfeld was successfully sued for libel by Khalid bin Mahfouz, a Saudi Arabian billionaire she had accused of funding terrorism. He took her to court in London, even though the book had not yet been published in the UK, and no more than twenty-three copies had been imported there. At the time, though, English libel law had a particular bias to the plaintiff, which his legal team exploited to the fullest. Since then, there have been efforts made to redress the balance, on both side of the Atlantic, but even just the sheer cost of mounting a full-scale legal defence, which can run into the millions, means that publishers and editors have often erred on the side of caution, and the stream of cases against journalists, pundits, even academic journals has continued.

This obviously has a chilling impact on freedom of speech and investigative reporting, but at least it essentially targets the victims' funds rather than their freedom. A particular modern approach with rather higher stakes is for governments to petition Interpol, the international policing information clearing house, to issue so-called Red Notices on their enemies. These are not, as is often assumed, arrest warrants as such, but are instead requests that police in the 194 member states arrest the individual in question for potential extradition. Interpol can refuse a request if it deems it politically motivated (albeit at the risk of alienating a country that helps pay its bills), and member countries have full discretion as to whether to pay attention to any specific ones of the more than 60,000 Red Notices in circulation. Nonetheless, being singled out in this way can have all kinds of implications, for everything from ease of travel to the chances of raising finance, so they make for excellent weapons against your critics and rivals. After a failed coup against him in 2016, Turkish president Recep Tayyip Erdoğan launched a wide-ranging campaign against his political opponents around the world using Red Notices. When Bill Browder, a businessman who fell foul of a corrupt scam in Russia, began openly criticising the Kremlin, he was hit by the first of several Red Notice requests. China and Egypt, Azerbaijan and Venezuela, Bahrain and Iran – authoritarian regimes around the globe have been using Red Notices, as well as extradition cases and other instruments of international law enforcement, as weapons against their enemies.

Is this warfare? To a large degree, it is the internationalisation of domestic persecution. However, we again come to the question of just what constitutes war. This allows repressive regimes and reprehensible individuals to reach into another country, ignoring their sovereignty – or rather, exploiting it – to exert their will. If, as some suggest, an assassination carried out by one state on a target in another ought to be considered an act of war, then why not the financial knee-capping resulting from a malicious law suit, or the invisible threat of a Red Notice, for which there is no appeal and which the target might only discover exists when they are pulled aside at passport control? In any case, such small-scale operations are very much at the skirmish level of the practice: there are whole seas and territories to be won through more ambitious adventures in creative lawfare.

LEGAL IMPERIALISM

The South China Sea is one of the most strategically significant stretches of water in the world. Falling broadly between China, Taiwan, the Philippines, Malaysia and Vietnam, it is a maritime crossroads between the Pacific and Indian oceans. Almost half as large again as the Mediterranean, half of global annual merchant fleet tonnage and a third of all commercial shipping passes through it, worth an estimated $3.5 trillion a year. Oil and gas fields stretch beneath it, and fish caught in its waters feed millions in South East Asia. Studded with reefs and wrecks, islands and archipelagos, it is also the subject of numerous competing claims from the seven littoral nations. Beijing has been the most aggressive in asserting its authority over the seas, even fighting skirmishes with Vietnam in 1974 and 1988. Although it periodically issues dark threats against the US Naval taskforces that periodically mount 'FONOPS' – Freedom of Navigation Operations – through Chinese-claimed international waters just to make a point, it has lately instead turned to lawfare to stake its claims.

The concrete manifestation of China's claims, no pun intended, has been its programme since 2013 to build and fortify islands in the South China Sea. By 2017, for example, it had both expanded existing islands and turned reefs and rocky outcrops into new ones, with a total area of 3,200 acres. Many of them have become military installations; the apocalyptically named Fiery Cross, for example, now has an airfield which can accommodate Xian H-6 bombers able to carry supersonic anti-shipping missiles. But their main significance is not so much military as political, part of a creeping extension of Beijing's claims across the sea and into disputed regions.

In 2020, for example, China formally began calling a vast stretch of sea down to the disputed Paracel Islands, east of Vietnam, 'coastal' rather than 'offshore', seeking to extend its national jurisdiction into international waters. Time and again, Beijing's gambits have been ruled out of order by international courts and arbitration, but it continues to use the forms and language of the law in what is nothing other than a naked land – sea – grab. So why do it? One of the great strengths of lawfare is precisely in the mind games it permits, confusing the issues, obscuring aggression and above all tying law-abiding states up in knots of their own making.

In practice, this is straightforward imperialism. However, Beijing has been smart enough to dress it up in judges' robes, fishermen's oilskins and coast guard blues. It presents a spurious but determined front of legality. Meanwhile, although it is garrisoning its new islands with regular military forces, the shock troops of this attempted conquest are seemingly innocuous. Fishing fleets are used to gather intelligence and above all stake implicit claims, because where China's trawlers go, so too do the ships of its Coast Guard and Maritime Militia, paramilitary formations that have become proxy military forces. They have clashed violently with those of other nations in protecting

China's self-claimed waters. In 2018–19, for example, Beijing sent 200 Maritime Militia vessels to contest the Philippine-occupied Thitu reef, deliberately blocking Manila's ships and all but challenging them to a first use of force that would have allowed the Chinese to present them as the aggressors.

It is perhaps unsurprising that it is Beijing which has so enthusiastically adopted lawfare in its campaign to assert control over the South China Sea. The first use of the term in this context appears to have been in *Unrestricted Warfare*, the groundbreaking book on strategy written by two Chinese military officers, discussed in Chapter 1. The genesis of modern international law was in the capitals of the West and in the wars they fought; to many beyond the West, it seemed that it was heavily skewed towards protecting Western interests. It must have seemed entirely fitting to turn such law into a weapon to confound the West and its allies.

BYPASSING BOUNDARIES

Certainly, lawfare has been adopted by other challengers. Russia is no less able and willing to weave a web of legalism around its empire-building. In the High North, for example, it has deployed everyone from geographers to submariners. It asserts that it owns a great wedge of the Arctic with an area of 1.2 million square kilometres (463,000 square miles), which happens also to be rich with oil and gas reserves. The basis of this claim is that, they say, this region is an extension of Siberia's continental shelf. The geography is questioned, the legal precedent dubious, but this has nonetheless allowed Russia to make a formal submission under the United Nations Convention on the Law of the Sea that has been running for years.

To reams of papers, annotated maps and geological studies, the Russians also added glitz. In 2007, special deep-diving submarines launched an exploration mission into the North Pole seabed. As well as taking water and soil samples, they left a specially made titanium alloy Russian flag. 'If a hundred or a thousand years from now someone goes down to where we were,' said explorer Artur Chilingarov, 'they will see the Russian flag there.' Other countries with their own Arctic claims hurried to say that this was just a PR exercise and gave Russia no special claims to the region. To no one's surprise, the Russian government later announced that the samples it had collected 'confirmed' that the disputed Lomonosov Ridge was part of Russia's continental shelf.

Does Moscow really believe it will be granted exclusive access to this stretch of the rapidly thawing waters of the Arctic and the riches beneath it? Probably not, but in the meantime it has headed off other claims, and done so in a way that makes an audacious heist look like a sober appeal to international law. Indeed, when Western countries discounted Russia's submarine gimmick, commentators in the postcolonial world grumbled about Western hypocrisy. The West had been happy enough, they observed, to steal their lands in the past with just such a flag-planting bit of theatre. Moscow was largely content: sometimes, a political victory is to be found in manoeuvring your enemies into shooting themselves in the foot.

At other times, though, the goal is more immediate and attainable. When the Soviet Union broke apart at the end of 1991, some 25 million ethnic Russians were left outside the borders of the Russian Federation, along with tens of millions of people who may not be ethnic Russians, but for whom Russian is their main language. This diaspora quickly became both a source of friction with neighbouring countries and also an asset to be mobilised, as Moscow claimed for itself a status as both leader of the *Russkii mir*, the 'Russian World', and also its protector.

To give this a kind of legal basis, Russia began issuing passports to disgruntled minorities abroad, typically in separatist regions at odds with their national governments: Abkhazians and South Ossetians in Georgia, Transnistrians in Moldova, the people of the Donbas in south-eastern Ukraine. When national governments try to crack down on rebels, Moscow then claims to be intervening simply to protect its own citizens, an excuse used when it fought a hard, fast, five-day war in Georgia in 2008, and in its running intervention in Ukraine since 2014. Of course, all nations reserve the right to defend their citizens – but by going out and actively offering Russian-speakers in potentially strategic territories citizenship in order to create the basis for interference, Moscow indulges in cynically creative use of this principle, which is, after all, the essence of lawfare.

LAWFARE CAN BE LAWFAIR

Of course, we must not be sanctimonious. While it tends to be revisionist, revanchist or downright repressive states that especially seek to use lawfare to their ends, the essence of law is that it is contested, and all states will seek to use it to their own ends. Israel and Palestine present the other as the aggressor in the International Criminal Court. US sanctions on Iran have been described as 'financial lawfare' because of the way they use courts and regulations. Indeed, the *New York Times* once said that 'President Obama's favourite combatant commander' was not one of his generals, but the Treasury under-secretary responsible for sanctions.

Ukraine, unable to dislodge Russia from Crimea by force of arms, has filed complaints in a variety of international courts:

the European Court of Human Rights, the Permanent Court of Arbitration, the International Court of Justice, even the International Tribunal of the Law of the Sea. It is not that it expects Moscow to be driven out by the 'borelords', but it at least hopes to generate political costs to the Kremlin by having multiple affirmations of the illegality of its annexation and the subsequent moves it has made to secure its new territory.

After all, lawfare is much about perception and reputation. One of the chief popularisers of the term was Charles Dunlap, at the time a US Air Force colonel and later general. He was concerned that it was being used by militarily weaker powers to 'handcuff the United States' and shift the field of combat from the battlefield and into the courts (and the court of public opinion) through spurious claims of atrocity and abuse. However, it is too easy to focus always on the ways that the cynical and the ruthless can exploit the strengthening of international law. However imperfect laws may be and however subtle and manipulative the lawyers that states can deploy, the solution is not to decide that law is not the answer. Laws may be a poor substitute for natural justice and right action, but they are, to be blunt, the best we have.

As the case of the MV *Alaed* at the head of this chapter demonstrates, used properly, lawfare can also be lawfair, deployed precisely to uphold the norms meant to shape the modern world, and also as alternatives to the good old-fashioned methods of armed coercion. Might may make right, but often in a very wrong way. However easy it is to disparage courts and lawyers, the role of the 'borelords' in curbing the excesses of the gangster, the kleptocrat, the tyrant and the terrorist ought not to be under-stated.

Sanctions – imposed and upheld by laws – can target such individuals, and at least bar them from entering states unwilling to turn a blind eye to their abuses. Measures such as Britain's still-underused Unexplained Wealth Orders, which freeze assets until their owners can demonstrate that they are not the proceeds of crime and plunder, can deprive kleptocrats of the very riches they crave. The war crimes tribunal in The Hague, the International Criminal Court, may be neither perfectly unbiased nor without unfortunate unexpected consequences – after all, leaders indicted there may be less likely to give up power, precisely because they face prison sentences when they do – but it nonetheless represents a consensus that some actions, from genocide to terrorism, are unacceptable in the modern world, and will be punished.

It's hard to be the good guy. Just as police officers may feel the temptation to plant evidence to ensure that someone they 'know' is a criminal gets convicted, so too even states which genuinely seek to be a positive force in the world will be tempted to shelve that idealism when pragmatism or profit beckons. But that is precisely why the law-based states have felt on the defensive of late, assailed by adversaries which either use their own laws against them or force them to choose between their ideals and the interests. The same US which Dunlap warned might be 'handcuffed' also found ways to use lawfare against insurgents relying on terror and the rule of the gun.

A central tenet of the US Army's *Field Manual 3-24 Counterinsurgency*, issued at the end of 2006, is that rule of law is 'a key goal and end state' because 'combat operations without civilian stabilization efforts are insufficient to "countering" or defeating an insurgency'. This doctrine, which became known as COIN, was meant to be applied in Iraq and Afghanistan. To be blunt, it failed – not so much because it was wrong, but because it wasn't given enough of a chance.

In Afghanistan, in 2010, Rule of Law Field Force – Afghanistan (ROLFF-A) was established under US brigadier general Mark Martins. It was to deploy teams on the ground directly to follow the conventional war-fighters into areas where the Taliban had been strongest. The idea was demonstrably to replace authoritarian and arbitrary theocracy with rights-based legality: anti-corruption initiatives, conflict resolution, transparent courts and policing. As observed by Jack Goldsmith of Harvard Law School, a key scholar of the subject, 'if that's not "using law as a weapon of war," I don't know what is . . .'

Six months later, a wider NATO Rule of Law Field Support Mission for Afghanistan was stood up. Six months after that, though, almost all the Rule of Law Field Support Officers were taken out of the field and concentrated back in Kabul. The experiment had not failed, but for political reasons – including resistance from some war-fighters who felt that these officers got in the way – it was essentially abandoned. However, this does show that it is possible. General Martins himself described it as 'affirmative lawfare in Afghanistan: a conscious and concerted reliance upon law to defeat those inside and outside of government who scorn it'. The lessons of ROLFF-A and 'affirmative lawfare' have not been forgotten. While hoping that the US does not find itself sucked into future messy counterinsurgency wars, even among the uniformed denizens of the Pentagon there are those who feel that next time, given that the US military already has a great deal of might, it will need instead to concentrate on the right.

WANT TO KNOW MORE?

Search for 'lawfare' and much of what you'll find is about US politics and free speech debates fought out in the courts. For the more geopolitical side of things, Orde Kittrie's *Lawfare: Law as a Weapon of War* (OUP, 2016) is, to be blunt, not the most exciting read, but it is very comprehensive. One of the best sources on the topic as a whole is the *Lawfare* blog (https://www.lawfareblog.com/), although it does cast its net very widely these days. On very specific cases, see Humphrey Hawksley's *Asian Waters: The Struggle Over the South China Sea and the Strategy of Chinese Expansion* (Abrams, 2019), Marouf Hasian's *Israel's Military Operations in Gaza: Telegenic Lawfare and Warfare* (Routledge, 2019) and Whit Mason's edited collection *The Rule of Law in Afghanistan: Missing in Inaction* (CUP, 2011).

CHAPTER 9

Information

Hillary Clinton ran her hand up Vladimir Putin's thigh, slowly, sensuously, and before we knew it, they were kissing with all the pneumatic abandon of teenagers – or porn stars. Because, I hasten to add, that is what they were. It was not how I had imagined the morning to start (I'd have had a lighter breakfast, if I had), but it was suitably attention-grabbing footage to kick off a briefing from an amiable team of wonks working for a European intelligence agency on the perils of 'deep fakes', video footage doctored with the use of advanced artificial intelligence combined with human artistry to show, well, whatever you want. In this case, it wasn't just that Clinton and Putin's heads had been superimposed onto footage of a couple of enthusiastic adult film actors, but that the images had been so seamlessly combined that, even knowing this was a fake, we could not spot tell-tale discrepancies or anomalies. Seeing really can no longer be believing.

This alliance of the high-tech and the highly tasteless was an especially vivid example of the new challenge of information warfare, driven by revolutions in how we create, consume and use media. We are, after all, now bombarded with information, disinformation, misinformation and infotainment. In large part, this is about the rise of the internet as a news source: as of 2019, 57 per cent of the entire global population used it, and 42 per cent were regular participants in social media. This has also made it ridiculously easy not just for states but for individuals to fake news: never mind artfully manipulated videos, you can just lie.

But it is also about how there seems to be a deep legitimacy crisis, as existing structures of government and assumptions about who we should believe, arguably products of the industrial age, come into question in the post-industrial, online era. As citizens and consumers, we find ourselves increasingly able to insulate ourselves in bubbles of news and opinion that flatter our assumptions and reinforce our prejudices. What's more, in an age of breaking news, instant hot takes and unmediated news feeds, we are drawn to the novel, the shocking and, as a result, often the unchecked, the exaggerated or the downright fake. A study led by Sinan Aral of the Massachusetts Institute of Technology, for example, found that 'it took the truth about six times as long as falsehood to reach 1,500 people' and that disinformation was 70 per cent more likely to be shared than real news.

No wonder unscrupulous actors, from peddlers of bogus erectile disfunction cures to hostile states, are eagerly exploring all the ways they can (ab)use the opportunities in the world of information. And, in fairness, no wonder that 'fake news' and (dis)information has become the moral panic of the age, the scapegoat for whatever developments we dislike, from the election of Donald Trump to 'wokeness', from jihadist radicalisation to Brexit.

This is a massive topic. There is outright disinformation, the deliberate spreading of lies, but there is also misinformation, the propagation of falsehoods by people who don't realise that this is what they are doing. Often, the problem is actually one of accurate information framed or contextualised in a misleading way or never intended for public consumption. Before the 2016 US presidential elections, Russian state hackers accessed emails in the servers of the Democratic National Committee and Clinton campaign manager, which they then leaked. This caused the Democrat leadership deep embarrassment, not least revealing their partiality for Clinton over her leftist rival Bernie Sanders. It contributed to a campaign to disrupt US politics and undermine Clinton, yet not with lies, but simply inconvenient truths.

The hack-and-leak is a growing problem, as we all have a tendency to be much less cautious in what we say in supposedly private contexts. In 2017, for example, while the small, rich emirate of Qatar was at diplomatic loggerheads with the UAE, emails of the UAE's ambassador to Washington, Yousef Al Otaiba, began to be leaked to US news outlets. He was soon being written up as a high-rolling playboy, a hypocrite, and maybe even corrupt. The UAE and its allies lost face diplomatically at the very time that they were trying to paint Qatar as a terrorist backer, and all without lies so much as, it is generally presumed, carefully framed and selected leaked emails.

Covering all this would take a book – indeed, has taken many books. Instead, in this chapter I want to sketch out some of the reasons why information warfare has become such a global concern, and what we might try and do about it.

FASTER, FAKER

Almost all of us – bar, perhaps, the North Koreans and a few lost tribes of Amazonia – now live in a single information space:

we can watch news from Qatar on our TVs (that's Al Jazeera, by the way), stream Russian videos on YouTube and even read stories cobbled together from foreign accounts gleaned from Twitter in the free newspapers we pick up on our commute. Perhaps more importantly, the old gatekeepers who decided, for the overwhelming majority of us, what we got to read, hear and see – newspaper editors and radio and TV channel directors – have lost their power. Now, not only can we tune into other networks and read other papers, but everyone with a Facebook page or Twitter account is, in effect, a media outlet themselves.

Indeed, while the age of the mercenary soldiers may or may not be returning, the age of the 'media mercenary' is definitely here. Diplomats, spin-doctors, journalists, pundits and writers, lobbyists, scholars, think tanks, NGOs and GONGOs (government-organised NGOs), these are the infowarriors. Thanks to them, we are bombarded with information – news, opinion, gossip, rumour, lies and revelations – at an ever-greater rate. Nor does this apply solely to those with smartphones and the internet, as even the traditional media have succumbed to the need to respond to the 24/7 news cycle, the desperation to be first to break the story and the inexorable eddies and currents of social media. Despite valiant efforts to preserve 'slow news' and the long read, it's a race to the swift.

This has certainly revolutionised the weaponisation of information. In the 1980s, for example, the Soviet KGB ran Operation Denver, a complex attempt to present AIDS as a US biological weapon. To do this, they first had to plant the rumour in a pro-Soviet Indian newspaper they had set up twenty years earlier through front organisations. This published an anonymous letter, ostensibly from a 'well-known American scientist', in 1983. It didn't get any real traction, so in 1985, an article citing the original Indian piece appeared in a heavyweight Soviet newspaper. The KGB roped in their Bulgarian and East German counterparts and the latter produced a pseudo-scientific report 'confirming' this story, ostensibly by a French researcher. Over the next few years, the myth would spread, but typically through stories planted in sympathetic (or sensationalist) newspapers abroad, magnified through the Soviet media, to try and simulate a groundswell of opinion. By 1992, reportedly some 15 per cent of Americans believed the virus was man-made.

That took years, a global network of agents, proxies and front organisations and a great deal of money and manpower. Compare that with a Chinese campaign in 2020. In mid-March, stung by accusations that poor food hygiene standards had led to COVID-19 and that it had concealed the initial outbreak, Beijing's infowarriors began suggesting that it was actually – again – a US bioweapon. Officials began tweeting and reposting accounts; conspiracy theory sites in the West gladly amplified it. So official spokespeople had to respond, and newspapers of record covered the story, even if only to dismiss it. Within days, the story had wormed itself into the global consciousness – and 29 per cent of Americans believed that the coronavirus had been cooked up in a lab outside China. Twice the result of Operation Denver, in days, not a decade.

NARRATIVES IN WARS

Old-style conflicts had war stories; modern ones are increasingly wars of stories. With conflict having pivoted from a physical act to a struggle fought in the imagination and collective will of society, information operations – or, as Nina Jankowicz notes in her aptly named *How to Lose the Information War,* what perhaps would best be called *influence* operations – are no longer just adjuncts to the kinetic, but often their replacements.

This is something that modern Russia seems to have understood especially well. Putin's Russia, believing itself locked in a conflict with a stronger West, which it regards as trying to deny it its rightful place in the world, has as a result become an especially eager adopter of these new forms of conflict. It sees in them a way to target what it considers the West's key weakness: that it is a constellation of democratic societies. As noted in Chapter 1, much ink has been spilt – wasted – on the mistaken notion that there is something called the 'Gerasimov Doctrine', a comprehensive Russian plan to use subversion, disinformation and military force to shatter Western societies. Rather, the Russians have, in effect, two separate approaches.

Chief of the General Staff Gerasimov's soldiers, like most modern militaries that plan for major and expeditionary wars, eagerly explore the ways that cyberattacks, propaganda, misinformation and similar sneaky tactics can support their regular military operations. There is nothing new in this. In the American War of Independence, George Washington's intelligence network spread disinformation about the poor morale of the Continental Army, lulling British Hessian forces into a false complacency, before the pivotal Battle of Trenton. In the Second World War, military deception became an art, with complex ruses constructed to misdirect Axis attention from the Allied landings in Sicily and Normandy. Now, though, there are simply vastly more opportunities to do it.

Russian businessman Evgeny Prigozhin has been placed under sanctions by the US, UK and EU alike for running both online propaganda-pushing 'troll farms' to perpetrate election interference, and also the mercenary company Wagner Group.

Wagner, in turn, is accused of pursuing Russian state interests in its role as private military contractor in various theatres of war. Prigozhin has denied any links with Wagner and dismissed the West's indictments against him. Kinetic and narrative conflict go hand in hand, though. In Libya, for example, Wagner is on the ground supporting General Haftar, Moscow's favoured warlord there, while all kinds of online disinformation have begun to crop up, clearly meant for Western consumption. Haftar is 'doing the Lord's work' in Libya, and is a 'fighter against jihad'. Whoever may actually be behind it, the aim is clearly to try and whitewash Haftar's image and encourage the West not to attempt to block his efforts to take over the country.

The Russian military itself has even more ingeniously disconcerting technologies at its disposal. Ukrainians fighting Russian troops and proxies in the Donbas found their cell phones pinging with messages appearing to come from fellow soldiers, saying 'Nobody needs your kids to become orphans' or 'We should run away', courtesy of a drone-based Leer-3 electronic warfare system able to hijack up to 2,000 mobile connections at once. Then again, the US Navy's forthcoming Netted Emulation of Multi-Element Signature against Integrated Sensors programme, NEMESIS (a cynic might suggest they came up with the cool acronym first, then designed the system) would spin the appearance of phantom fleets of ships, submarines and aircraft in the ether. From subversion to misdirection, soldiers are entering a new world of chaos and uncertainty.

DISRUPTION, DISRUPTION, DISRUPTION

Then there is a second, arguably more significant approach. While Russia's soldiers explore how to use influence operations to tilt the balance on the battlefield their way, the Kremlin's national security team seems to have decided that they offer a way to win without needing to get involved in shooting wars at all. In what looks strikingly like Kennan's aforementioned 'political war', updated for the twenty-first century, this means using manipulation, disinformation and misdirection to achieve national goals without firing a shot. As General Gerasimov put it in his fateful article, 'the role of nonmilitary means of achieving political and strategic goals has grown, and, in many cases, they have exceeded the power of force of weapons in their effectiveness'. It says something when a die-hard tank commander suggests that information operations may be more powerful than his heavy metal.

Putin's agenda of reasserting Russia's status as a great power does not require him to expand its borders (except for Crimea – that was, in his eyes and those of most Russians, simply taking back something stolen from them in 1954), but it does set him against the West. From his point of view, anything that divides, distracts and demoralises us is useful. So Moscow encourages secessionism from Scotland to Spanish Catalonia, cheers on populists and extremists from left and right with even-handed malice, and does everything it can to magnify tensions within and between nations.

This included supporting Brexit, Britain's painful withdrawal from the European Union. But these influence campaigns don't appear actually to influence the outcomes in any significant way: even the narrow 52-to-48 per cent Brexit victory cannot, the evidence suggests, be ascribed to Moscow's meddling. The Scots voted against independence (that time), attempts to meddle in elections in Continental Europe backfired in most cases, and the election of Donald Trump in 2016 seemed to catch the Russians by surprise. Convinced Hillary Clinton was going to become president, and fearful that she would prove a dangerous enemy, the Kremlin had simply been backing every divisive alternative and stirring up every disruptive cause, from anti-capitalist radicalism to gun-rights fundamentalism. (I appreciate this will be a controversial view for many, who see Trump as Putin's choice of president – all I can say is that everyone in Moscow political circles I talked to before the elections did not believe for a moment he *could* be elected, and they didn't seem to exert themselves to try and secure his re-election in 2020.)

Disruption, after all, is a more achievable and more reliable goal than some kind of Manchurian Candidate-style covert takeover. Whereas the Soviet Union was at least partially constrained by its Marxist-Leninist ideology, today's Russia is devoid of any credo beyond its own nationalism. It can support left and right, radicals and traditionalists, big business and anti-capitalists, all at the same time. And it does.

During the Second World War, Winston Churchill memorably said that 'in wartime, truth is so precious that she should always be attended by a bodyguard of lies'. These days, inconvenient truths can also be mobbed by a hit squad of lies, generated and propagated by state media, online trolls and proxies alike. When Malaysian Airlines flight MH17 was shot down over the Donbas in 2014, by a Russian-backed militia unit using a Russian-supplied missile, Moscow's information warfare machine went into overdrive generating alternative narratives – in this case, a euphemism for outright lies – for what had happened. As of mid-2020, the EU's s East StratCom Task Force had identified more than 260 different stories, from the idea that the plane was shot down by a Ukrainian jet to, most audacious of all, that its 298 passengers and crew were already dead, corpses stuffed into a plane deliberately blown up over the Donbas as a provocation.

Time and again, this tactic has been employed, from the attempt by Russian military intelligence officers to poison double-agent Sergei Skripal in the UK in 2018 (His daughter did it! It was a British plot to stop Russia hosting the football World Cup!) to the poisoning of opposition activist Alexei Navalny in 2020 (He was drunk and took pills! It was the CIA!). The aim of what the Russians call *infoshum*, 'info-noise', is not so much to persuade people of one line or another as to raise a fog of falsehood, to make it seem impossible to know what is true and what is false. In the process, it becomes all the easier to disrupt other countries and to undermine their will and ability to act with decisiveness.

NARRATIVE WARS

Is this just a Russian dark art? Not at all. Let's be honest: everyone does it, at least to some extent. Just as the difference between determination and pig-headedness is often in the eyes of the beholder, so too it is often difficult to distinguish in practice between the propaganda of the other side and our own 'strategic communications'. That doesn't mean that everyone is the same, though. Consider the big state-funded international TV networks. Russia's RT, the China Global Television Network (CGTN) and Iran's Press TV may present themselves as the same as the BBC, Voice of America (VOA) and Germany's Deutsche Welle, but they are not. The difference is really in the states themselves: the former all regard themselves at being at narrative war, and demand a wartime level of media mobilisation. Objectivity, balance, a willingness to see the other's point of view – these seem to be luxuries that a wartime state cannot afford. Propaganda, after all, always marches behind war, whether overt or not.

RT began in 2005 as a relatively high-quality TV network, with a national agenda, to be sure, but not necessarily that far off that of the BBC World Service, VOA or France 24. As the Kremlin came increasingly to see itself at virtual war with the West, though, so too did RT. When editor-in-chief Margarita Simonyan was asked in 2013 why Russia needed RT, she said, 'for the same reason the country needs a defence ministry' – that is, in case it finds itself in an information war. One cannot wait until a war has started to arm, was her rationale: the military is always ready, just in case, and 'so are we'.

Now, the remnants of high-quality news sit uneasily alongside toxic rants and programmes providing platforms to conspiracy theorists and fringe extremists. Russia's draft 2020 state budget included 23 billion roubles (£235 million or $300 million) for RT. By contrast, VOA's 2020 ask was for $190 million. But we ought not exaggerate its actual impact. In the UK, for example, its peak viewing figures struggle to reach those of S4C, a Welsh-language TV network. No wonder it so often seems perversely delighted by alarmist Western assessments of its influence, as it likely scrapbooks them to try to convince the Kremlin they are worth the money after all.

Still, the Russians are not alone, even if there are different models. China's CGTN, for example, doesn't seem to have quite the same mission as RT. Its standards are no higher, as exemplified by its broadcasting of the 'confession' of a British journalist charged with bribery after he had been intimidated, drugged and handcuffed to an iron chair inside a cage. However, Beijing is less interested in 'info-noise' and trying to obscure inconvenient truths and is instead eager to buy positive coverage. In Africa, for example, it has spent a great deal of money creating media outlets that reportedly maintain two editorial teams. Locally recruited journalists and editors have considerable leeway, right up until a story has particular significance for China. Then, editors in Beijing step in to 'advise' – rewrite, reorient or reject – as they see fit, to ensure that Chinese policy is treated in appropriately enthusiastic terms.

Likewise, many actors employ covert influence operations, sometimes using Russia's tactics, sometimes their own. While Moscow used trolls and other social media gambits to try and sow discord during the 2016 US elections, for example, Tehran was trying to promote specific talking points, inciting disapproval of Israel and Saudi Arabia. It especially used Riyadh's (genuinely terrible) human rights record as the basis for a campaign questioning continued American support.

China, by contrast, focuses on ethnic Chinese abroad and is generally reckoned to be less effective in the 'fake news' stakes, but nonetheless has been targeting Taiwan in particular. In 2019, for instance, it pushed a video by a journalist that, to a jarringly poppy soundtrack, claimed that Taiwanese president Tsai Ing-wen was selling the country to Japan. This was hyped by a government-sponsored group on Weibo, a Chinese social media platform: Diba. Russia has its online trolls, employees working for organisations such as the notorious Internet Research Agency, who pump out deceptive social media to contract. By contrast, Beijing has Diba, a network of enthusiastic patriots and mischief-makers happy to spread pro-government memes and ferociously attack government critics at home and abroad.

After all, these narrative wars are not confined to hiding truths or spreading propaganda, they are also about silencing inconvenient voices. In 2019, the *National Enquirer* ran stories about an extra-marital affair by Jeff Bezos, CEO of Amazon but also owner of the *Washington Post*. Bezos's security team said that it was Saudi retaliation for the *Post*'s coverage of the Khashoggi murder, that the compromising information was collected through spyware installed on his phone – and they noted he had swapped numbers with Prince Mohammed Bin Salman only a few weeks earlier.

DEFENCE AGAINST THE DARK ARTS

However much Western governments may grumble about 'fake news', most do not consider themselves in the midst of narrative wars, or at least do not think that they are truly problematic, and thus they do not seriously fight them. There is much that can be done. But many of the remedies are expensive, politically controversial or, for the politicians (who themselves deploy dark narrative arts of their own), downright inconvenient.

There are technical responses, such as unleashing artificial intelligence to find and delete suspicious social media posts. The hope that what technology has done, it can undo, though, is still likely a vain one. Algorithms may identify automated trolls, for example, but are we willing to let them censor newspapers?

There are regulatory options, seeking to place a greater duty of care on platforms. Arguably, while these companies have been claiming to embody a new culture of responsibility, we should treat this with some scepticism. Social media companies are essentially transnational, substantially beyond the reach of any national laws. More to the point, they profit from fire and fury, from toxic online spats and viral conspiracy theory: these mean clicks, and clicks mean money. Besides, asking them to decide what is fact and fiction is again a dangerous step, given that much so-called disinformation is actually minority opinion or mis-contextualised truth. In an age when debate can be characterised as microaggression, how are we to cope with situations in which what appears to be inaccuracy is presented simply as opinion? A socialist's truth may be a neoliberal's fake news, and vice versa.

The irony is that it is authoritarian states, which demand a 'sovereign internet' whereby they can control the news and opinion their citizens can access, that are the closest to being in a position to do this. To defend ourselves against 'fake news', are we really willing to accept Chinese-style online censorship? And if so, who decides what gets censored?

Then there are political responses, often generated by a simple desire to be seen to be doing something – anything – rather than grounded in evidence of real effectiveness. Governments typi-cally love 'mythbusting' organisations that seek out and counter ostensible falsehoods, not least because they lend themselves to the bureaucratic mindset: you can plot metrics and claim success through activity rather than impact. After all, the evidence is that these rarely work. If anything, they can actually reinforce fake news. I remember talking to a Czech activist of what could charitably be described as fringe views (NATO was planning war against Russia, for example, and Eurocrats in Brussels planned to ban the Czech currency). He was repeating a tale that the Czech Interior Ministry's Centre Against Terrorism and Hybrid Threats had recently debunked. He sat back and sipped his beer, clearly relishing the moment. With the confidence of a man holding all the aces, he added 'if it were not true, why else would They' – the portentous capital T was obvious – 'be so desperate to deny it?' How does one argue with that kind of logic?

None of these approaches offers more than partial and temporary relief (if that). Instead, the deep solutions are neither easy nor quick. Governments and political classes that themselves have become addicted to empty promises and cheap slanders must work at relegitimising themselves. Electorates, though, cannot claim to be the innocent victims here: we have too often and for too long indulged the mountebanks and elected the tricksters. We get the governments if not that we deserve, then certainly that we choose, and in the process we lay ourselves open also to manipulation and disruption from abroad.

In order to hold our masters' feet to the fire, and to minimise the impact of foreign influence operations, we need to know when we are being hoodwinked, bamboozled and generally manipulated. Media literacy is as vital a survival skill in the new age as sex education and first aid. The conventional wisdom is that it needs to be taught at school, and that is right – but unless we are willing to wait twenty-plus years for a newly savvy generation to become voters and candidates, it also must be extended to the rest of society.

Disinformation is often described as viral, and it does spread in a strikingly similar way. The metaphor works both ways, in that 'information hygiene' can help stop it spreading. Fadi Safieddine of the University of East London, for example, found that if just 30 per cent of social media users check to see if a post is accurate before re-posting it, that can help stop it from spreading, much like people practising social distancing to scotch coronavirus. Rather than debunking it after the event, 'pre-bunking', giving people the skills and the understanding of the wicked world of information warfare, is the best way to vaccinate us all.

Information

It's not sexy, it's not easy, it's not quick. It also will mean a very uncomfortable new world for deceitful politicians, over-selling advertisers and all the other hidden and overt persuaders. It is, however, the difference between fixing the leaky roof on your house and putting out buckets and opening an umbrella every time it rains.

WANT TO KNOW MORE?

There is a particular genre of quick and dirty, headline-chasing 'information warfare' books, typically pegged to some contro-versial event, especially the rise of Donald Trump, which charac-teristically grant the villains of the piece – usually Russians – almost magical powers of mind control. Fortunately, there are also sensible studies that neither over- nor under-play the issue. Although information operations are only part of what the Soviets and then Russians have called 'active measures', Thomas Rid focuses on this aspect in his *Active Measures: The Secret History of Disinformation and Political Warfare* (Profile, 2020), and does it very well. Nina Jankowicz's *How to Lose the Information War* (I.B. Tauris, 2020) is more upbeat than it sounds and has great lessons from the front lines of this conflict. *War in 140 Characters: How Social Media is Reshaping Conflict in the Twenty-First Century* (Basic, 2017) by David Patrikarakos and *Likewar: The Weaponization of Social Media* (Houghton Mifflin Harcourt, 2019) by P.W. Singer and Emerson Brooking cover broadly similar territory, but both have insights to complement the other. Finally, Peter Pomerantsev's *This is Not Propaganda* (Faber & Faber, 2019) is a very readable and personal guide to the new world of subjectivity and make-believe.

CHAPTER 10

Culture

Our hero dispatches enemies by the dozen with gun, knife and fist. He catches a rocket-propelled grenade in the coils of a spring mattress. He plays chicken with tanks. Rambo? No. James Bond? Hardly. It's Leng Feng, Chinese special forces super-soldier and star of the gloriously over-the-top Wolf Warrior films. And in his climactic show-down with an American merce-nary, who tells him that 'people like you will always be inferior to people like me; get fucking used to it', Leng retorts 'that's fucking history', and promptly kicks the stuffing out of his arrogant Anglo antagonist.

America may have invented the gung-ho blockbuster, but, as with so much else, the Chinese are catching up fast. In *Wolf Warrior II* (2017), its highest-grossing film to date, Leng Feng, now cashiered, takes on the savage mercenaries of the fictional US 'Dyon Corps' in Africa led by 'Big Daddy' – subtlety is not its strongest suit – over their attempts to steal a new cure for a terrible disease. In the finale, People's Liberation Army Navy destroyers blast mercenary tanks with long-range missiles and pin-point accuracy. At the end of the film, superimposed over a Chinese passport, is the reassuring bombast: 'To citizens of the People's Republic of China, when you find yourself in danger in a foreign country, do not give up hope. Please remember, behind your back, will be a strong and powerful motherland.'

And just in case the message wasn't clear enough, in the following year's blockbuster, *Operation Red Sea* (2018), Chinese commandos save 130 of their citizens from evil jihadist terrorists in Yemen, sorry, the fictional 'Yewaira', who were also, just in case the viewer didn't realise how nasty they were, planning on using a radioactive 'dirty' bomb. Once all the pyrotechnics had died down, the viewer was meant to be left in no doubt but that China is a global power – at the end of the film, its ships warn off US Navy vessels – and that Beijing will look after its people, wherever they may be.

Well, maybe. At least as long as they aren't Uighurs, pro-democracy campaigners or whistle-blowers. In fact, China has not been especially active in rescuing its own citizens kidnapped or arrested abroad. Even so, it is a powerful statement of super-sovereignty, reminiscent of the unconscious arrogance of Lord Palmerston, when the British Empire was at its height, affirming that 'a British subject, in whatever land he may be, shall feel confident that the watchful eye and the strong arm of England, will protect him against injustice and wrong'.

CULTURAL POWER

Power is about perception, influence about imagination. Empires long understood this, and one could argue about the extent to which cricket, Christianity and the chance to say the words *cives Romanus sum*, 'I am a Roman citizen', were as powerful as force of arms in building and preserving them. During the Cold War, with direct US–Soviet conflict frozen by the threat of mutual nuclear destruction, sport and ideology became new battlegrounds: America's 4–3 ice hockey victory against the Soviet reigning champions in the so-called Miracle on Ice game during the 1980 Winter Olympics was even at the time touted by some commentators as a fitting rebuke for Moscow's recent invasion of Afghanistan.

Today, culture is a growing arena for contestation. Its effect is often subtle, and is as much about convincing one's own population to spend the blood and treasure to be assertive abroad as directly undermining enemies. But who is winning? When the star-bedecked and red-flag-wrapped Soviet model that once promised egalitarianism, enthusiasm and a leapfrog into industrial modernity was shown to offer corruption, repression and stagnation, the 'West' seemed for a while to be the future. In popular culture, Hollywood and 'CocaColanisation' – the globalisation of the American consumer lifestyle – ran the board. Foreign tourists in Soviet hotels would be accosted by black marketeers eager to buy their Levi's, and when the first Pizza Hut opened in Moscow, people queued up for five hours for this supposed fast food, willing to pay the equivalent of a week's wages for what was, quite literally, considered a taste of freedom. Other imperial powers found their own ways to turn cultural capital into soft power, from Britain's lasting image as the bastion of justice and fair play (though Tony Blair's cringe-worthy attempts to rebrand the nation as 'Cool Britannia' never took off) to France's attempt to monopolise chic.

Increasingly, though, there are new challengers, who are combining economic progress with confident cultural outreach –

above all, in Asia, where Bollywood and K-pop represent this new soft power for India and South Korea respectively, and where China is trying to find a cultural dimension to its growing economic and military might. But from jihadist beheading videos to computer games, new forms of cultural power are emerging everywhere, and new players are entering the game.

How does cultural warfare really work, though? It is not as though a song has ever brought down an empire or started a war, is it? No sports contract can make annexation acceptable, just as no video game can transform a pacifist into a warmonger. Well, no, that's true – but they can certainly help.

CAN A SONG BRING DOWN AN EMPIRE?

The stolid commissars of the Soviet Union once feared that Western music was being weaponised to subvert their youth, and they may have been right. There is a fascinating story about the power ballad 'Wind of Change' (1990) by the West German band Scorpions. It became something of an anthem of the revolutionaries who brought down the Berlin Wall and with it the East German regime in 1989, and then of anti-communists through the rest of the Soviet bloc. The claim is that it was supported and maybe even written by the CIA. This is denied by the band, but it is not wholly implausible, given that the CIA had already engaged in cultural influence operations from printing and distributing Boris Pasternak's epic and critical novel *Dr Zhivago* in Russian to sending copies of Arthur Koestler's searing anti-Stalinist book *Darkness at Noon* over the Iron Curtain by balloon.

In the previous chapter, I addressed the impact of information and misinformation, but cultural messaging can likewise spread subversive values or undermine national will. For example, South Korean NGOs (sometimes with the implicit sanction of the government) also send balloons floating into North Korea with everything from bibles to leaflets, CDs of banned films to radios, all to break Pyongyang's censorship. *Hallyu*, the 'Korean wave' in culture, has been explicitly denounced as a weapon in North Korea, where it is referred to as *Nampung* (the 'Southern Wind').

Likewise, tensions between India and Nepal in 2020 ended up on the airwaves as Nepal – whose army is not even one-fifteenth the size of its neighbour's – began broadcasting critical messages into India through transmitters erected on hills near the border. Earnest declarations of Nepal's case do not necessarily make for the most compelling listening, though, so instead they also broadcast a new genre of songs combining popular folk melodies with lines such as 'Dadagiri chhor Bharat' (Stop bullying, India) and 'Lutiago humro bhoomi' (Our land has been stolen). In response, some Indians have begun circulating jingoistic memes about their country's claim to the disputed territories.

The very term 'jingoism' suggests that wars can come from a snappy chorus. The Russo–Turkish War – another of many Russo–Turkish Wars – had broken out in 1877, the result of risings against Ottoman rule in the Balkans and tsarist desires to combine protecting Christians from Muslim over-lords with a nice little land grab. Having already been bloodied in the 1853–56 Crimean War, the British government was unde-cided how best to act. There was concern about Russian expan-sion, and Queen Victoria herself was worried that this might be a prelude to an attempt to wrest control of the 'jewel in the crown' of the empire: India. At the same time, Liberal party leader William Gladstone had done much to arouse anger at the Ottomans' treatment of Balkan Christians, notably with his pamphlet *The Bulgarian Horrors and the Question of the East* (1876), and there was little sympathy for the Turks.

Then along came 'The Great MacDermott', a popular music hall singer who, for one guinea, bought a song with the rousing chorus 'We don't want to fight but by Jingo if we do,/We've got the ships, we've got the men, we've got the money too,/We've fought the Bear before, and while we're Britons true,/The Russians shall not have Constantinople.' It became a massive hit; even the Prince of Wales, the future King Edward VII, had him sing it at a private audience. A population for whom the war had been a distant spat of little interest became righteously patriotic. The political balance was tipped, and a fleet was duly dispatched to force Russia to terms.

The power of such left-field cultural interventions is not that they force a reluctant state into action. It is, rather, that they can be mobilised to win internal political disputes over whether to act. The boisterous chorus of the nineteenth-century music hall has given way to online video and Twitterstorms, but the same principle applies. For example, the documentary short *Kony 2012* (2012) about the eponymous Ugandan war criminal and cult leader empowered those who had been trying to push the US into adopting a more assertive stance and the African Union to send troops against his Lord's Resistance Army. In 2014, Sony Pictures was hacked, and among the files accessed was the yet unreleased *The Interview*, a black comedy in which two journalists are granted access to Kim Jong-un and then recruited by the CIA to assassinate him. Pyongyang (likely behind the hack) expressed its fury, and even threatened terrorist attacks on any cinemas which dared show the film. Its fear seems to have been two-fold: that even fictional representations of a spiteful and self-indulgent Kim being assassinated might encourage similar attempts inside North Korea, or that it could create a ground-swell for some kind of direct action against the regime by the US. The thought that a comedy might have such an impact may seem far-fetched, but it later emerged that not only had an expert from the independent-but-government-adjacent RAND Corporation been consulted beforehand (he advised to keep the scene where Kim is killed, as it might 'start some real thinking in South Korea and, I believe, in the North'), but also the Assistant Secretary of State for East Asian and Pacific Affairs. Life and art can be more closely connected that we might think.

CAN A LICENSING DEAL WHITEWASH A NATION?

Of course, national opinion is a contested space and is frequently influenced, maybe even shaped, by external forces. China, for example, knows that it faces rising fears about its economic and military power and global ambitions, and seeks to prevent concrete actions to constrain them. It's up to you whether you consider this a cunning ruse to disarm a gullible world or a sensible bid to defuse hysterical 'Sinophobia'.

This is not just about offering foreigners cheap Mandarin classes and bankrolling domestic cinema, though they also do that. (In 2020, it emerged that Germany's largest book chain may have been paid to prominently showcase such page-turners as President Xi Jinping's series of collected speeches.) Having long engaged in systematic censorship at home, Beijing is increasingly seeking to censor global debate on issues it considers embarrassing or prob-lematic. In 2019, Daryl Morey, general manager of the Houston Rockets basketball team, tweeted support for pro-democracy protesters in Hong Kong. The tweet was quickly deleted, but not quickly enough. The Rockets, until then the most popular American basketball team in China, was blocked from state TV. The National Basketball Association had affiliated itself with a range of progressive positions at home, but its relationship with China was going to be worth billions over the next few years, and so it moved quickly to appease Beijing. Morey was publicly rebuked and disowned; pro-protest signs were confiscated at televised games; players were told to refrain from commenting on Chinese policy. Freedom of expression, it appears, should not get in the way of business.

A combination of economic muscle, ruthlessness and organised facsimiles of expressions of popular outrage are allowing Beijing to police its image in the global square. In 2020, Taiwanese and Chinese activists using such established terms as 'communist bandit' or '50-cent party' (a term used to mock trolls working for Beijing) in comments on YouTube found them being automatically deleted within 15 seconds. YouTube subsequently said this was because of 'an error with our enforcement systems', but suspicions still linger that either the company wanted to avoid angering Beijing, or else there had been an organised campaign to game the systems which respond to public complaints. The so-called Great Firewall has long censored politically sensitive terms and topics for domestic users; this would represent an attempt to export that kind of information control.

The aim is quite simply to make any response to various potentially objectionable Chinese policies, from the suppression of its own Uighur Muslims and Hong Kong democrats to the annexation of Tibet and possible tardiness in publicising the COVID-19 outbreak, unthinkable simply by making them unmentionable. As one American diplomat told me, 'we're nowhere near that stage yet, but the Chinese intention seems not to make what they're doing look right, so much as to erase from public debate everything they're doing that's wrong'. She added that 'if that happens, it's going to be harder than ever to persuade people to accept the costs of any showdown'.

CAN A GAME MAKE YOU FIGHT?

Even if the chorus is singing jingo, you need to have 'got the ships, and got the men, and got the money too'. To contest the globe, whether through political war or economic pressure or outright force, you need both the resources and the will. This is a challenge that is fought at home, and increasingly again through film and television, viral videos and computer games.

There is, after all, a reason why the Pentagon started backing films fitting its agenda as early as 1927. Then, Army Air Corps pilots and planes were provided to help make the war film *Wings*, which went on to win the very first Academy Award. Gung-ho representations of US military glory may well earn a producer the chance to use real locations and even kit. For the sequel to the Tom Cruise testosterone-fest *Top Gun* (1986) – *Top Gun: Maverick* (2020) – the filmmakers were granted the use of F/A-18 jets, even access to a Nimitz-class nuclear aircraft carrier at, in effect, cost. In return, the Pentagon got the right to make sure its 'messages' were reflected in the film . . . and an exclusive preview screening for the top brass. Furthermore, since 2002, the Pentagon has been financing the various iterations of the *America's Army* computer game and distributing it for free. Why? As the developers themselves said, 'we want the whole world to know how great the US Army is'.

Of course, much of this is for domestic consumption. The original *Top Gun* has been hailed as the greatest recruiting asset for US naval aviation ever, just as nowadays the US military has its own e-sports team playing the *Call of Duty* computer game competitively to attract applicants to the real thing. The overwhelming majority of the *Wolf Warrior* films' box office take was in China. The producers are looking for profit, but the states that back such patriotic cinema are seeking to ensure their forces have the recruits they need and a public willing to see them put in harm's way.

The US may have traditional dominance in this field, but even in gaming this is being challenged. The big contemporary games franchises such as the aforementioned *Call of Duty: Modern Warfare* duly exalt Western military strength and feature antagonists from Arab terrorists to Russian ultra-nationalists. However, others have come to appreciate the potential in this pyrotechnically addictive medium. In 2003, the Lebanese movement Hezbollah released *Special Force*, a first-person shooter game in which the player took on the role of a militiaman fighting the Israel Defence Forces. (In a telling indication of how their priorities shifted, a successor released in 2018, *Sacred Defence*, cast Islamic State militants in Syria as the enemy.) Meanwhile, since 2002, Syrian-based company Afkar has produced its own shoot-'em-up games with a distinct political stance: *Under Ash* (2002) and *Under Siege* (2005), in which the enemies are again Israelis. Whether specifically to groom a new generation of fighters, as Hezbollah undoubtedly hoped, or simply to challenge the perceived bias of the genre, as Afkar claimed, the point is that cultural conflict has moved into this realm, too.

DARK POWER

What happens if you can't define the public imagination, as expressed through these media? In *Rocky IV* (1985), the eponymous all-American fighter, Sylvester Stallone's Rambo of the boxing ring, lines up against Ivan Drago, a chilly, drug-enhanced Soviet killer. In the distant sequel *Creed II* (2018), Drago is drilling his son to be an equally remorseless fighter for a demolition match in Moscow. Cold War stereotypes have simply been spruced up, oligarchs replacing commissars, and Vladimir Putin emerging to many as the ultimate Bond villain stepping from the screen and into real life.

It is not as if the Russians haven't also sought to earn soft power. Consider the money and effort put into ensuring that both the 2014 Sochi Winter Olympics and the 2018 World Cup went so well. It was not just a classic Soviet-style chance to show off the prowess of (sometimes drug-enhanced) Russian athletes as a metaphor for a virile and powerful state; it was also to try and undercut narratives of nasty Russians. Both events were well run and showed Russia at its imaginative and even welcoming best. However, with poisoners running amok in London and Salisbury (defector Alexander Litvinenko dying of radioactive polonium in 2006, MI6 asset Sergei Skripal narrowly escaping death by Novichok nerve agent in 2018), 'little green men' popping up in Crimea in 2014 and gangsters and hackers working hand in glove with the Kremlin's spies, it is perhaps inevitable that the effect of such events was limited. The bad guy image endures. However, in a perverse way, the current Russian regime appears to be making something of a virtue, even a strategy, of a necessity.

Don't think you can sell yourself as the good guys, or the plucky upstart? Then maybe it's worth turning, as it seems Putin's Russia has, to what is in many ways the counterpoint to soft power, the 'dark power' of presenting yourself as too dangerous to be worth messing with. After all, making yourself look like the biggest, baddest bully in the schoolyard is another narrative victory of sorts, and can be mobilised to deter resistance and leverage concessions.

Time and again, Russian policy seems almost calculated to cause offence and make itself look unpredictable and menacing. In 2014, for example, Denmark was debating whether to be part of a NATO anti-missile defence system, and Finland was even considering joining NATO (in which case, Sweden would likely have followed suit). There were, though, voices at home which warned that this might actually put them in greater jeopardy, and Moscow clearly wanted these voices heard. According to the Danish Defence Intelligence Service, at the very time that the country's leadership, including Prime Minister Helle Thorning-Schmidt, was in Bornholm in June 2014 for a regular political festival, the Folkemødet, Russian warplanes simulated a nuclear attack on the island. Two missile-armed Tu-22M3 Backfire supersonic bombers, escorted by four Su-27 Flanker fighters, cut across the Baltic Sea at low level before turning back just before entering Danish airspace. A radar station on Bornholm had spotted them and scrambled Danish F-16 fighters, but had this been real, they would not have been able to intercept the attackers before they launched.

The following year, Russia staged a major military exercise involving 33,000 soldiers, rehearsing how they would not just take Bornholm but head further and invade mainland Denmark, Sweden, Norway and even Finland. Does Moscow actually have territorial ambitions in Scandinavia? Almost certainly not. However, simply by wargaming such aggressive scenarios, the Russians were seeking to make a point as to what might happen to the countries of the region if they 'provoked' Russia. In 2015, the Russian ambassador to Copenhagen, with all the subtlety of a mafioso demanding protection money, warned that, if Denmark joined the missile defence system, 'it would be less peaceful and relations with Russia will suffer. It is, of course, your own decision – I just want to remind you that your finances and security will suffer.' In 2016 Putin himself rhetorically asked the Finns whether they thought there would be no consequences to their joining NATO: that while his troops had been withdrawn to positions away from the common border, 'do you think they will stay there?'

Ultimately, Denmark decided not to be part of the missile defence network, 'as the result of a broad review of political and security factors'. And Finland is not in NATO.

In his *Discourses on Livy* (1517), Niccolò Machiavelli argued that it can be 'a very wise thing to simulate madness'. US president Richard Nixon infamously used this as a strategy in the Vietnam War, letting both the Soviets and the North Vietnamese believe he was so obsessed with ending the conflict one way or the other that he might use nuclear weapons. More recently, much of North Korean signalling also appears designed to hammer home the notion that it is not a 'reasonable' state, and that it will respond in disproportionate, even counterproductive ways if threatened (even by a mediocre film, it seems).

Bullying and pressuring your way in the world can work in the short term (ask the Danes), but in the longer term, there are serious downsides to a strategy that makes you an outsider whose word cannot be trusted and whose very existence poses a threat. This is why such signalling is often the preserve of those who have nothing to lose, either nations that are already pariahs, like North Korea, or terrorist pseudo-states. The horrific beheading videos circulated by al-Qaeda, Islamic State and other jihadist groups, for example, are intended to be both warnings and also signs of their absolute determination. A handful of sociopaths may be attracted to the cause, but the idea is that those who are aghast will also be left with an abiding assumption that these are enemies so fanatical that surely it is impossible to beat them. Whether this works is another matter, but captured and intercepted jihadist communications make it clear that this is part of the thinking behind this macabre theatre. A bomb in a marketplace, a politician gunned down in the street and a chilling video: these are all, precisely, messages of terror.

WINNING THE CULTURE WARS

As with the (dis)information issue, liberal democracies need to be true to themselves. While our politicians love to present themselves as the champions of our values, their statecraft rarely matches their rhetoric. It is difficult convincingly to champion democracy and liberalism in Russia, Venezuela and North Korea while for so long having cheerily allowed China and Saudi Arabia not only to flout the same values at home but to persecute those espousing them abroad.

There is a huge opportunity for a serious and sustained new cultural – and thus political – counterattack to the new authoritarianism that is increasingly evident around the world. This does not mean 'our' propaganda to combat 'theirs', if propaganda is taken to mean falsehoods, exaggerations and artful omissions. In the heyday of US cultural imperialism, its ability to sell the American Dream depended, of course, on more than a little sugar-coating, but it genuinely reflected an enthusiasm, optimism and sincere belief that this was a message of hope to all. These are, though, rather more cynical and self-reflective times, and it is harder to avoid the uncomfortable truth that freedom and prosperity for some has too often been bought at the cost of exploitation for many and ecological devastation for all.

It is not that propaganda, censorship, bombast and jingoism cannot work; it is that they are dangerous and often destructive tools. A cultural counteroffensive needs not just resources, but also the right tone. Better to be humorous than to hector, to lead by example rather than exegesis. Once, it was possible to try and market a nation and a way of life through celluloid alone. Now, films can be juxtaposed with news footage, and everyone can Google any factoid to see if it is true. While it may be that we will be happy to live in invented worlds that flatter our prejudices, it may also be that authenticity will reacquire a weight of its own. In other words, if we are to try and convey a positive message about ourselves, we have genuinely to live it first.

Of course, it could be that this is a challenge that will resolve itself, that we will not only gain the media literacy to see through disinformation but also begin to push back against weaponised culture. Consider the live-action remake of the Disney epic *Mulan* (2020), a big-budget blockbuster-wannabe filmed in China and heavily influenced by Beijing's interests. Some of the changes are essentially details, such as excising a love scene that apparently scandalised the cultural commissars, but more generally, this has been turned into Chinese nationalist propaganda with a glossy, Americanised veneer. It was even shot in Xinjiang, where a million Uighurs languish in concentration – 'retraining' – camps, and the credits thank the local branch of the Public Security Bureau, China's infamous political police.

And the result? The film was a box-office disappointment both globally and within China, and Disney came in for considerable criticism. Winning the cultural wars is a lot harder than it may seem, and even patriotic epics can be counterproductive at worse, short-term 'sugar rushes' at best. As with the use of information, credible authenticity will likely become all the more important in an age when everything can be faked, and states that may seek to project influence through culture will find this works best when those values and attitudes are genuine.

WANT TO KNOW MORE?

Popular Culture, Geopolitics, and Identity by Jason Dittmer and Daniel Bos (2nd edition, Rowman & Littlefield, 2019) is an engaging and thoughtful primer on how representations can influence the world they represent. Nancy Snow's *Propaganda, Inc.: Selling America's Culture to the World* (3rd edition, Seven Stories, 2010) focuses especially on the US Information Agency, while Eric Fatter's *American Empire and the Arsenal of Entertainment* (Palgrave Macmillan, 2014) is broader. The story about 'Wind of Change' was explored in a fascinating and engaging podcast of the same name (Pineapple Street Studios/ Crooked Media/Spotify, 2020).

PART IV

Welcome to the Future

CHAPTER 11

Weaponised Instability

It's a different day after tomorrow, and French commandos and German hackers are about to bring the chaos. Frogmen from CPEOM, the maritime component of the Action Division of France's foreign intelligence service, the DGSE, lower an unmanned underwater vehicle – a deep-diving drone – into the water from an apparently innocuous fishing boat. It stealthily makes its way to the fibre-optic cable emerging from the sea bottom (close to the shore, they are buried for safety) and lays an explosive charge, then returns to the ship, no one any the wiser. As the commander of the operation helps secure the drone, a thumbs-up from one of the sailors lets him know that the other team has also accomplished its mission. It was a matter of delicacy, after all: the charges were laid not to cut the cables directly so much as to trigger shock waves that would break them indirectly. Even a cursory inspection would show this, but the aim was deniability, not secrecy.

Meanwhile, in the picturesque Bavarian town of Dillingen an der Donau, the hackers of the 292nd Information Technology Battalion, part of the Bundeswehr's new CIR cyberwarfare command, were finishing uploading malware into the airport's computers. These had been recently updated, and would have been resistant against most malicious hackers, but not against tools that had been developed with all the resources of a state behind them.

The target is not Russia or Syria, Libya or Iran, but fellow NATO- and EU-member state Italy, and the final weapon will be an emissary from Brussels, slightly rumpled after her early morning flight into Rome. She bears a secret but nonetheless deadly serious ultimatum for a populist new government that seems to think it can go ahead with 'Italexit' at the risk of destabilising the euro and triggering the potential dissolution of the European Union. Her message is quite simple: if you thought the troubles that faced Britain when it went through Brexit were bad, this is as nothing to the chaos that would grip Italy. To make the point, at the moment she stepped through the doors of the Foreign Ministry's elegant Farnesina Palace, the two cables connecting Sardinia to the World Wide Web out of Olbia and Cagliari were cut. Across the island, downloads froze, emails stuck in outboxes and banking communications stopped, while system administrators scurried to reconnect via satellite links. Meanwhile, computers at the island's main airport at Cagliari suddenly went down, leaving air traffic controllers desperately redirecting inbound flights to the smaller fields at Alghero and Olbia.

It was a carefully calibrated warning. Sardinia accounts for less than 3 per cent of Italy's population and just 2 per cent of its GDP. No one died, and no permanent harm was done; repairing the cables would take a few weeks and purging the airport's systems maybe a day, but then all would be back to normal. It was not enough to seriously hurt Italy, and if Rome wanted, it had the face-saving option of explaining it all away as extreme misfortune rather than enemy action. But it was also enough to make a point about what can happen when the interconnectivities that underpin modern life and economies are challenged – whether by political gestures or covert operations.

IS THE MOUSE MIGHTIER THAN THE SWORD?

A far-fetched and even Europhobic fantasy? Of course. There are many countries more prone to use covert violence and pressure than others, less constrained by international law or public opinion demanding better from them. Germany is not the same as China, France as Iran. Yet allies have already threatened economic sanctions against allies (the US on Europe over the Nord Stream II gas pipeline in 2020), spied on each other (Turkish agents have been uncovered in fellow NATO states from Britain to Denmark), spent millions lobbying each other (according to the Center for Responsive Politics' Foreign Lobby Watch, in 2018 it was not Russia or China who spent the most on political lobbying in the US but South Korea, Japan and Canada), tapped fellow leaders' phones (it seems likely that the NSA listened to Germany's Angela Merkel until 2013) and even backed rival proxy armies (France and Italy are supporting one side in the Libyan civil war, Turkey the other). If that's how allies treat each other, then, while we are admittedly fortunately still a long way from EU members mining each other's internet cables, it is hardly surprising how bare-knuckled wider political and economic competition can be.

In part, this is precisely because the modern world is free both of the controlling strictures of the Cold War – when the superpowers, to a degree, could decide which conflicts would be permitted and which controlled – and of the danger of full-scale inter-state war. As discussed in Chapter 2, such conflicts are becoming less common, both for positive reasons such as the saliency of international law, but also because they are getting too expensive in economic as well as political terms.

The Human Security Report Project has been tracking the trajectory of conflict for years. According to their data, between the early 1990s and the end of the 2000s the overall number of conflicts fell dramatically, with an almost three-quarters decline in the kind of vicious wars that kill at least a thousand people a year. After 2010, they began reporting a distinct spike in global war death tolls; drawing on Uppsala University's Conflict Data Programme, the Project reckoned that the figures soared by 600 per cent between 2010 and 2014. In the main, though, these were conflicts in which Islamic extremists were involved, and they were at least partly civil wars. Besides, it was only temporary: from 2014, these 'battle deaths' were back in decline, even in the Middle East, which accounts for the overwhelming majority. Most wars continue to be intra-state affairs, uncivil ones of brother against brother, sometimes with foreign involvement, sometimes largely not.

Of course, none of this means that there will be no more inter-state shooting wars. Sometimes, bad luck, bad blood or bad calculations will mean that those pricy new weapons or trusty old ones get an airing. (That reliable veteran, the AK-47 rifle, has killed vastly more people than nuclear bombs or any other 'weapons of mass destruction', after all.) In 2020, Syria, Libya and Yemen continued to burn, the on-off war between Armenia and Azerbaijan over the disputed enclave of Nagorno-

Karabakh flared up again, and Chinese and Indian soldiers brawled in the high mountains of Kashmir. Nonetheless, in most cases there was a clear desire from most parties to avoid wider escalation. Indeed, in Kashmir, both sides eschewed guns for stones, knives, and sticks wrapped with barbed wire – murderous, to be sure, but deliberately intended to prevent the border conflict slipping out of control.

So is the world getting any safer? Not so much. There is a whole academic industry devoted to assessing how many wars are being fought and how many people have died in them, but the trouble is that, as with so many academic industries, it often becomes dominated by disputes over definitions. What is a war, what is a major conflict? Does a child starving because civil war has disrupted supply chains count? A battle-scarred veteran who commits suicide after demobilisation? A terrorist killing in the name of a distant conflict, or a gang war over the local turfs in which to sell drugs from the other side of the world? Internal conflicts – civil wars, insurgencies, clashes between heavily armed criminal organisations – are more common than ever, and the aggregate toll in lives ended, blighted and ruined remains high. Again according to the Conflict Data Programme, 2018 saw the highest level of battle deaths from non-state conflicts, and the collateral toll is equally high. Countries may not be warring against each other, but the world remains a dangerous place.

FLY-BY-WIRE SOCIETY

In part, this is just the bloodstained evidence of a wider challenge. The culmination of many of the processes and practices described in this book is an increase in instability within countries and within the international system in general. Much of this is not purely accidental. I do not mean that some shadowy cabal of conspirators is behind it, so much as that instability is often the flipside of dynamism and even responsiveness. It may seem a stretch to compare modern society with an advanced aircraft, but an angular, sawtooth jet such as America's F-117 Nighthawk or Russia's brand-new Su-57 'Felon' is specifically designed to be unstable. Once, this was a recipe for a quick crash, but modern computer systems constantly monitor the aircraft's movements and adjust its control surfaces to maintain controlled flight, vastly more quickly and more accurately than any human pilot could. An unstable aircraft is more responsive, manoeuvrable and efficient than a stable one – so long as the 'fly-by-wire' control systems keep working.

Instant communications and unmediated media, cross-border supply chains, just-in-time logistics (whereby stocks are kept as low as possible, replenished on the basic of projected need), computerised and algorithm-driven share trading, trans-national corporations able to pick and choose between tax and regulatory jurisdictions, global crime networks and equally global memes: all these have undermined old models of social, political and economic governance without putting anything in their place. The traditional state, the patriarchal family unit, the press barons and network bosses: all such institutions are under pressure, either failing or adapting, even if at the moment we don't know what they are changing to.

Global society is not a victim of these processes; it is largely their beneficiary and certainly their accomplice. The unstable fly-by-wire nature of the modern world has liberated hitherto shackled or marginalised human capital, lifted populations out of poverty, galvanised technological change, generated massive economic growth and allowed new communities to form that span the globe, from online gaming clans to the ad hoc networks that form to provide funds and practical aid when disasters strike. Between 1998 and 2018, global life expectancy at birth rose from 67 to almost 73 years, and the proportion of the world's population living in absolute poverty fell from 32 per cent in 1995 to 10 per cent in 2015. This is a time of revolution.

In the following, final chapter, I will turn to some of the ways in which, rather than just surviving the weaponisation of everything, we may find it can also benefit us. Of course, though, there is no escaping the downsides of this instability. Populists and secessionists drink deep of the font of fake news and conspiracy theory and are invigorated and empowered therefrom. Narrative conflicts divide communities and bring the legitimacy of existing systems and polities into doubt. Economic pressure fosters corruption and impoverishes those whom it does not enrich. Neoliberal economics have set the market free, and the market has rushed across the borders and freed itself from much national control, in turn. Law becomes a weapon, not a shield. At the extreme end, warlordism rears its ugly head, sometimes overtly, such as in North Africa and Afghanistan, but elsewhere taking more urbane guises, with the rise of mercenaries, corporations with armies of private security, and regional authorities asserting their control over local police and paramilitaries. There is a generalised legitimacy crisis across the globe, taking different forms in different regions; yet even this is not just a result of the new age of non-kinetic war but also a new opportunity for it.

GEOPOLITICS AS A 'SPECIAL OPERATION'

Despite the occasional venture into deniable and proxy operations, which in any case soon are admitted or unmasked, it is essentially pretty obvious when two nations are at war in the conventional sense. There is fighting, there are deaths. There are incentives to make an open declaration of war – that way your soldiers have rights under the Geneva Convention – and at the same time there are clear constraints under international law.

But what happens when all the seething rivalries, misunderstandings, traditional enmities and political machismo embodied in inter-state competition are not vented through the medium of war? In 2018, Andrei Kortunov, director general of the Russian International Affairs Council, liberal scholar and former diplomat, gave a sober warning of the consequences of the 'victory of the paradigm of war over the paradigm of politics, over the paradigm of diplomacy' and 'the expansion of a military mindset to non-military aspects of world politics'. He was speaking at a meeting of the Valdai Club, a gathering of Russian and foreign experts that culminates in a set-piece appearance by Putin himself. Kortunov continued:

> They say that all means are fair in love and war, including disinformation, deception, and provocation. But this should not be the case in politics, where reputation, predictability and reliability are very important. . . . It seems that we all – in East and West – are beginning to live according to the laws of wartime, when all means are good, and reputation becomes an unaffordable luxury or, at least, an easily spent resource. And as a result, for example, a very important red line between politics and a special operation is practically erased.

A 'special operation' – in other words, an intelligence agency mission – may have become the new paradigm. After all, the blunt truth is that even allies spy on each other. In the rare cases where there are 'no spying' agreements, then they find ways round them. They may rely on 'espionage-lite' activities such as diplomatic contacts, open-source analysis and outsourced operations (including contracting out intelligence gathering to consultancy firms that have their own sources in the other country). Or they may do it indirectly. The MUSCULAR internet surveillance programme operated by Britain's Government Communications Headquarters (GCHQ) and the US National Security Agency (NSA), sucks up data on millions of email communications around the world, allowing tracking of communications even between allies. Or they may simply look for loopholes. Although under the terms of the treaty that created the Commonwealth of Independent States among many of the post-Soviet states Russia's Foreign Intelligence Service (SVR) agreed not to spy on fellow members, military intelligence and the domestic FBI-on-steroids Federal Security Service (FSB) simply stepped into the gap, because they aren't covered by the agreement.

So even friends spy on friends, and especially when it comes to the inevitable economic competition between them. European Commission officials have suggested British intelligence was deployed to access their documents and discussions over Brexit negotiation strategy in 2018. Countries such as France, in which one of the four divisions of the DGSE is specifically dedicated to economic intelligence, have been especially active in supporting their national champions with aggressive intelligence campaigns. Their activities range from cyberespionage (the US's 2013 National Intelligence Estimate listed France alongside Russia and Israel as the main second-rank threat in this respect, behind China) to old-fashioned methods such as breaking into executives' briefcases. The aim is to turbocharge domestic research and clinch export contracts, and where the French go, their main competitors are inevitably tempted to follow. They are hardly alone: in 2015, for example, Austria alleged that the NSA spied on its defence firms, and Germany uncovered similar operations against Europe's multinational Eurocopter consortium. In 2020, it was the turn of the Danes to allege NSA snooping on their and Swedish industries. Nor are information operations, where strategic communications blur into psychological war, a Russian, Chinese or Iranian monopoly. At the end of 2020, for example, Facebook shut down a network of accounts being secretly run by French military intelligence, promoting its military presence in Africa.

Intelligence operations are thus ubiquitous and constant, regardless of alliances and formal treaties. They are directed towards protecting all aspects of the national interest, whether detecting and resisting hostile subversion or helping win a major trade deal or conclude a treaty. They involve everything from hacking to physical intrusion, cultural contamination to outright violence. An individual operation may be compromised, cancelled or concluded, but the intelligence wars are neither declared nor ever truly ended. Is there a better metaphor for the new world of inter-state conflict?

NO WAR, NO PEACE

It would be nice to think that the genuinely global threats that face us – not least climate change – would likewise mean a new, global mindset. The trouble is that human beings are complex beasts, able to cooperate wholeheartedly for one cause while still completing fiercely on another. Consider, for example, the response to another and more immediate global challenge: the

SARS-CoV-2 or COVID-19 coronavirus pandemic that raged across the world in 2020. There has been genuine international solidarity, with alliances to share vaccine research and medical data, and commitments to assist poorer countries to access medication. There has also been bitter international recrimination, finger-pointing and occasional veiled suggestions from countries less badly hit by the virus that their status reflects their national virtues. It has been alleged that Russia and China have turned to espionage to try and win the 'vaccine race' and reap the consequent political and even economic gains. Meanwhile, America attempted to use its economic muscle to corner the market in the drug Remdesivir and even protective equipment: allegedly, officials literally turned up at Shanghai airport with suitcases of dollars to intercept a shipment of surgical masks originally bound for France.

It is tempting to put our hopes in a reinstitution of a now increasingly mythologised former stability, but it is also clear that this was actually a temporary phenomenon and largely a by-product of the Cold War. The First and Second worlds of West and East maintained their apparent stability those days at the cost of that of the Third, which became the playground for proxy wars. The Cold War was rather hotter in Vietnam and Korea, Afghanistan and Angola, Nicaragua and the Middle East. This 'stability' was also underwritten by the mutual terror of thermonuclear annihilation. It is questionable whether we would really want to return to that, even if we could.

So the alternative may be to embrace the opportunities of instability and the ways that it can be a dynamic, even positive, force. Companies able to be nimble enough can arbitrage the uncertainty. In the words of one corporate executive, political risk analysis was once about avoiding disaster, but now it has become the route to making money. States can exploit the flexibilities of an unstable order. The art is, as one British diplomat put it to me, 'not allowing instability to equal mayhem' but rather 'to appreciate that this is another word for dynamism and opportunism, in which we need to balance self-interest with wider moral concerns'. That's the challenge to which we turn finally because this book, like Pandora's box, hopes to bestow hope at the end.

WANT TO KNOW MORE?

There is no lack of texts on the present unruly – and unruled – state of the world. *The New World Disorder: Challenges and Threats in an Uncertain World* (Lexington, 2019), edited by J.L. Black, Michael Johns and Alanda Theriault, is a weighty collection of essays but impressive in its breadth of issues covered, from the Balkans to Brexit. Peter Zeihan's *Disunited Nations: The Scramble for Power in an Ungoverned World* (Harper, 2020) is more opinionated, and none the worse for that. Of course, it is also worth reading alternative perspectives. Although Francis Fukuyama's thesis has been as reviled as it has been misunderstood, his *The End of History and the Last Man* (Free Press, 1992) remains one of the best examples of a school of thought that sees democracy and peace as an inevitability, just over the horizon. For a counter-blast, try Amy Chua's *World on Fire: How Exporting Free-Market Democracy Breeds Ethnic Hatred and Global Instability* (Arrow, 2004), whose title says it all.

CHAPTER 12

Learning to Love the Permanent, Bloodless War

It was 1364, and the city-state of Florence was at war. A merce-nary army engaged by neighbouring Pisa, led by the English soldier of fortune John Hawkwood and the Rhinelander Hanneken von Baumgarten, was advancing towards the city, having looted the subordinate town of Pistoia on the way. Against them, Florence mustered under a condottiere merce-nary captain of their own: Galeotto Malatesta. They met on 28 July at Cascina. Despite being caught by surprise, Florence carried the day, not least thanks to a contingent of Genoese mercenary crossbowmen armed with the latest, steel-bowed weapons. It was a bloody day's work, though, with hundreds of casualties and perhaps as many as two thousand Pisans captured. Yet meanwhile, 65 kilometres to the east, in Florence, one could be forgiven for thinking the blood was not staining Cascina's fields under a pitiless summer sun. The men of finance were standing behind their green-clothed tables – the 'banchi' from which comes the word 'bank' – changing money and making loans. The sculptor Alberto di Arnoldo was making the final touches on the Madonna and Child with Two Angels that would crown the door to the Loggia del Bigallo. In the winding alleyways between the Old Market and the Baptistry, their usual neighbourhood, the city's prostitutes were displaying their charms. In short, while their soldiers were fighting and dying, life went on as usual for the Florentines.

Of course, it helped that so many of 'their' soldiers were mercenaries, from somewhere else. Malatesta himself came from Rimini, on Italy's eastern coast, and had fought for Naples and Sicily before the Florentines and would go on to serve first the Byzantine emperors and then the Pope in Rome. Besides, while cities could be besieged and looted if the tide of war turned against them, otherwise conflicts were – before the hammer blow of French invasion at the end of the fifteenth century that began sixty-five years of devastation – often relatively limited, fought on others' territories. The mercenary commanders, whose soldiers were their bankable asset, tried to fight wars of manoeuvre, where the aim was to out-think and out-march the enemy into a hopeless position, to avoid pitched battles that would bleed each other white. Meanwhile, princes and magnates competed to demonstrate their cultural authority and wealth by commissioning great art and instructing heralds and historians to create the right kinds of narratives.

NOT THE TIME OF THE CUCKOO CLOCK

The parallels are not at all exact but nonetheless thought-provoking. For most 'northern' nations – Europe, North America, Russia – the overt military conflicts in which they are involved are largely wars of choice, wars from which they can walk away. They are fought 'over there', from the Middle East to

Africa. There are casualties, but largely among professional soldiers who are generally deemed by public and politicians alike to have chosen the risk when they chose the life (even if for many the range of alternative options might not have been that broad). Often, though, the wars are fought with proxies, from drones and genuine mercenaries to allied forces and militias; as Andreas Krieg and Jean-Marc Rickli argue in their 2019 book of the same name, this is the age of 'surrogate warfare'.

Likewise, the covert and civil conflicts fought with sanctions and cinemas, lawyers and spies, are surrogate wars in another way, transferred into new battlefields. In all cases, there can be blowback when the wars go badly: the families mourning a soldier fallen on a foreign field, the terrorist bombing, the economy suffering under sanctions, the public debate getting more toxic thanks to judicious encouragement. However, most of the time, the wars seem distant and life goes on as usual, just as it did for the Florentines.

What is more, these conflicts are often not only distant but covert, and as a result undeclared, unacknowledged, even unrecognised. And what is never openly begun is likewise rarely officially ended. Instead of a comfortingly simple war/peace binary, one that was always less cut and dried than we might have wanted to believe, we are heading into an age when everyone may be in at least some kind of a state of 'war' with everyone else, all the time, and it is just a matter of degree. Of course, we will still have allies and enemies, but these terms will mean different things at different times, in different contexts. Our very vocabulary is outdated: war, enemy, victory, all these concepts need to be re-thought. Welcome to a potential world of permanent, sublimated conflict, of the political struggle of all against all.

The sooner we recognise this and adapt, the better our chances of avoiding such a situation – or the better we will do in it. After all, it may be disconcerting to face this future of constant competition, but there are also opportunities and virtues in this age of bloodless battles, calibrated coercion and outsourced opposition. If the parallel is the Renaissance, then we ought to remember Orson Welles's possibly unfair but undoubtedly memorable line in *The Third Man* (1949): 'In Italy, for thirty years under the Borgias they had warfare, terror, murder and bloodshed, but they produced Michelangelo, Leonardo da Vinci and the Renaissance. In Switzerland, they had brotherly love; they had five hundred years of democracy and peace, and what did that produce? The cuckoo clock.' These are definitely not cuckoo clock times.

INTERNATIONAL INSTITUTIONS: NEW RELEVANCE?

Properly addressing responses to the new world of war would take a book in itself, but it is worth sketching out some of the ways that different aspects of modern society can respond in positive ways, to minimise harms and maximise opportunities. It may appear that there is no place for international institutions such as the UN, for example, but arguably the opposite is true. It is, rather, that the focus needs to shift away from a concentration on 'big war' and towards setting and enforcing the new 'etiquette' of international relations. The Organisation for the Prohibition of Chemical Weapons (OPCW), for example, has come to the fore, following chemical weapons attacks in Syria and the use of the Novichok nerve agent in the attempted poisonings of Sergei Skripal in 2018 and Russian opposition leader Alexei Navalny in 2020. The OPCW's very strength is its

210

specificity: it is purely dedicated to the permanent and verifiable elimination of all chemical weapons, in line with the 1997 Chemical Weapons Convention. It can muster world-class expertise, a set of powers defined by the Convention and considerable global authority. Russia has been blamed for these attacks, seemingly tried to hide remaining stockpiles from the OPCW and eventually sent a team of hackers to try and break into its computer systems wirelessly from a nearby carpark. For all that, even Moscow still accepts its mandate.

As the notion of inter-state dispute blurs out into the weaponisation of so many other areas and issues, from law to criminality, intellectual property disputes to social media algorithms, the challenge will not be to try and outlaw these conflicts – how is this possible? – but rather to manage and moderate them. Existing bodies, such as Interpol, the International Court of Justice, the World Health Organisation and even the International Telecommunication Union (the UN agency responsible for everything related to information and communication technologies) will have to raise their game to adapt to these new challenges.

While in the short term this may seem difficult, not least because those countries most eagerly employing new forms of inter-state conflict may be reluctant to limit their options, it is a challenge seen and overcome before. For example, in the nineteenth century, Britain and the US were reluctant to see the expanding 'dumdum' bullet banned because they valued its use against so-called fanatical tribesmen in India and Africa, and the Philippines, respectively. Nonetheless, they accepted its banning as a weapon of war in the 1899 Hague Convention. In part, this was to avoid seeing them used against their own men, in part because of international pressure and domestic opinion.

Welcome to the Future

As for such fiendish devices as napalm and plastic shrapnel that cannot be detected by x-ray, the intimidatingly named 1980 Convention on Prohibitions or Restrictions on the Use of Certain Conventional Weapons Which May Be Deemed to Be Excessively Injurious or to Have Indiscriminate Effects was meant to put paid to them. Now, there is active talk at the UN about a cybersecurity treaty, and suggestions that the 1936 International Convention on the Use of Broadcasting in the Cause of Peace and the 1953 Convention on the International Right of Correction can be repurposed to address disinformation. In short, while it is fashionable to decry international law and its conventions, it continues to chase the challenges.

Besides which, why can the good guys not use some of these new options? How about openly and transparently using smart, targeted propaganda to undermine regimes defying international law, and doing so strictly sticking to the truth and not being tempted to exaggerate and misrepresent? How about more aggressive efforts to freeze and seize the funds of the corrupt, the abusive and the murderous? We hear much about the use of missile-firing drones to fight wars and hunt terrorists, but unmanned aircraft are also becoming staples of humanitarian operations: monitoring ceasefires, delivering medicines to remote locations, fighting forest fires and spotting boatloads of refugees. So too, the institutions of the international order are not moribund, not doomed only to be abused, but instead need to be adapted to more positive uses in the new world of war.

They also need to be protected from deliberate marginalisation. China has been adopting an interestingly subtle strategy. Instead of trying to break the institutions of the international order and attacking them head on, it has instead begun to create an alternative suite of structures that begin by shadowing and even complementing them, but with the potential eventually to pose a challenge. When nations can pick and choose between rules and institutions, then they become not citizens of the world but consumers. The Shanghai Cooperation Organisation, founded in 2001, is not an Asian NATO, but nonetheless seeks to be the continent's primary security institution, and as Russia is a member, it already stretches into Europe. The Asian Infrastructure Investment Bank is always keen to work with the World Bank and the International Monetary Fund, but in the process is creating a Sinocentric process that pushes not just Beijing's interests, but its values, too. The debate over the Trans-Pacific Partnership trade accord is telling; US president Barack Obama warned that 'we can't let countries like China write the rules of the global economy. We should write those rules.' These are all about who shapes the future. Trade deals that dilute protections for intellectual property and place less emphasis on environmental sustainability; security agreements that put more emphasis on national security than human rights; political frameworks that exalt national sovereignty over common global understandings: these all could define the next global era, if Beijing gets its way. The irony is that the Chinese are the true Westphalians now, but their desire to sideline the current international order does nonetheless demonstrate how these institutions really matter.

THE STATE: NEW TOOLS?

Let's say you have $15 billion burning a hole in your pocket – what would it buy you? You could get a new Ford-class nuclear-powered aircraft carrier, and maybe its complement of aircraft, but you couldn't actually afford to put it to sea, let alone assemble the accompanying battle group of escorts and support ships needed to ensure that you haven't just bought a huge and expensive target. After all, the Chinese Dong Feng DF-21D or Russia's new 3M22 Tsirkon hypersonic missile are clearly considered carrier-killers.

On the other hand, it is equivalent to the financial aid package with which Vladimir Putin persuaded Ukraine's then-president Viktor Yanukovych to make a U-turn and abandon his plans to sign an agreement on closer cooperation with the EU at the expense of its relationship with Russia. To be sure, that fateful decision in 2013 triggered Yanukovych's downfall, but the principle stands. Alternatively, it could pay the World Health Organisation's bills for three and a half years, underwrite three-quarters of the UK's entire overseas development aid budget for a year, give 3,000 key foreign officials a $5 million bribe, or offer 100,000 smart young people from around the world, the next generation of entrepreneurs, politicians and influencers, 4-year scholarships to study in your universities and become exposed to your culture.

How far are security and influence fungible assets? While 'big wars' may be in decline, shooting wars are not wholly a thing of the past, and any country that relies purely on influence and covert coercion might find itself wishing it had kept some guns and missiles in its arsenal. However, at a time when new military technologies are forever being hailed as the new big thing, the systems that will reinvent war (although in practice nothing looks set to replace the Poor Bloody Infantry sitting in a foxhole as the fundamental building block of all battles), many nations are facing some tough decisions about where to put their money.

In 2021, for example, the UK unveiled its Integrated Review of Security, Defence, Development and Foreign Policy, billed as a comprehensive assessment of the country's threats, needs and strategic opportunities that would break new intellectual ground. Even so, it had already been determined that Britain would retain its nuclear forces and continue to commit to spending at least 2 per cent of its GDP on defence (once the pandemic spending crisis was over). So this was not a completely blank sheet exercise. The risk was inevitably that it would end up as the usual reallocation of marginal resources rather than anything truly groundbreaking. Indeed, much of it turned out to be just that, even if dressed up in the predictable rhetoric about 'a problem-solving and burden-sharing nation with a global perspective'. Nonetheless, the UK does deserve genuine credit for at least recognising that this kind of exercise was necessary – most countries have not even got this far, yet. All governments tend to be conservative, and individual armed services, ministries and other institutions will naturally fight to retain and expand their budgets, that being the main mark of success in a bureaucracy.

In the future, nations will need to be increasingly imaginative and flexible in how they think about power, international influence and their security, though, and for those states able to achieve this, the opportunities are considerable. Estonia, for example, is a tiny country whose population is smaller than that of Munich or San Diego. Nonetheless, the experience of being hit by Russian cyberattacks, as well as a commitment to pioneering digital e-government, has made it a powerhouse for both cybersecurity and, though this is much less widely touted, cyberespionage. You don't have to try and outspend America's NSA (whose estimated 2020 budget is only marginally below that of the entire Estonian state) to build niche capabilities that depend on smart individuals given scope to, well, weaponise their smartness.

In the past, there were small countries such as Jordan and Iceland that acquired disproportionate global influence thanks to their strategic location, and others thanks to leveraging the political muscle of diaspora populations (including Ireland and Israel). In the future, countries may be able to punch above their weight if they develop and retain such niche capabilities. Poland discovered that, by sending members of its GROM special forces unit to take part in allied operations in Iraq and Afghanistan, it acquired unexpected levels of influence and access in Washington and beyond. A military force became a political asset. Other countries have long cultivated economic edges, from Luxembourg's bank secrecy to Singapore's business-friendly regulatory environment, which can be converted into geopolitical muscle. Now, new opportunities are arising. Since 2008, the Republic of Korea has been committed to an ambitious programme of low-carbon green growth, not just in response to the impact of climate change and pollution on the country itself, but also to become a global workshop for these technologies, and it is devoting some 2 per cent of its GDP to this end. This is, of course, good for the world and good for South Korea – including in new security terms. By taking an early lead in emerging green technologies, Seoul is calculating on reaping the economic rewards, which can be reinvested into other sectors (including maintaining its hefty defence spending, which accounts for around 2.7 per cent of its GDP, compared with the European average of 1.7 per cent). It also calculates that this will give it a disproportionate political voice, as countries vie to take advantage of its new intellectual properties.

Learning to Love the Permanent, Bloodless War

Larger countries that seek to cover every base may well find that it doesn't matter if you have the latest fighters or even lots of soft power if your infrastructure is especially vulnerable to hackers or your political elite is susceptible to unchecked bribe-taking and foreign influence. Nigeria and South Africa, for example, are the richest and notionally most powerful nations in Africa, yet hamstrung by corruption and instability, their capacities to develop are limited by these invisible constraints.

This will also raise a fundamental question for nations, just as it will for the international system: what is the value of values? It is easy to see this new world as one belonging to the cynical, but fortunately it is not quite so cut and dried. One of the greatest vulnerabilities of many modern states is actually the mismatch between rhetoric and reality. Politicians and insti-tutions trumpet their adherence to values-based policies, from Sweden's 'feminist foreign policy' to, as the Britain's Foreign, Commonwealth & Development Office's mission statement puts it, demonstrating 'the UK acting as a force for good in the world'. This is all very well, so long as the language matches, and is seen to match, the reality. Sweden's commitment to gender equality in the world has been admirable – but it sells arms to less-than-woke Saudi Arabia, for example. 'Force for good' Britain still punches above its weight in the world, but according to most indices has seen its soft power decline of late, especially because of a perception that Brexit reflected insu-larity and generated institutional disfunction.

This is not to single out these countries – every progressive initiative tends to have its points of failure – so much as to high-light the challenges in balancing mass and morality, relevance and righteousness. Especially in domestic policy, it is precisely this gap that tends to provide the weaknesses that other states can exploit. From public mistrust of official sources opening them up to disinformation to a lack of transparency and accountability encouraging corruption and the funding of disruptive political movements, we ourselves define the threats we face. A free, pluralistic and accountable press; proper transparency of beneficial ownerships and political donations; a serious commitment to human rights abroad and defending the sovereignty of other states; proper media literacy and penalties for platforms abusing the right to free speech; uplifting economically and socially marginalised communities at home and nations abroad – none of these is in the slightest bit revolutionary, but doing more of them, more consistently and more enthusiastically, would help.

After all, closing the gap and actually living up to our own grandiose rhetoric, at home and abroad, might be hard, but ultimately will generate both authority (Sweden has a population of just 10 million, but in soft-power terms tends to be ranked in the world's top 5 or 10) and security. And, yes, spending that $15 billion on bribes abroad may look like a smart move, but remember: at best, bribes do no more than rent people, and what you pay them today, you'll have to pay them again tomorrow. What's more, if those become the accepted rules of the game, how will you stop your own officials from being bribed as easily by a more deep-pocketed rival?

THE PRIVATE SECTOR: NEW MARKETS?

It is tempting (and often fashionable) to cast the private sector as a jackal feasting off the entrails of international society. It is certainly true that the outsourcing and universalisation of inter-state rivalry is creating all kinds of new commercial opportunities.

It is not just a good time for mercenaries and corporate spies: film-makers, spin-doctors, lawyers, programmers, money launderers, all kinds of entrepreneurs can get a cut of the action. It is naïve and unfair to condemn all this as immoral profiteering, though, as many companies explicitly seek to work for their home nation, or do internalise some kind of moral code.

That last point is a crucial one. In a transnational age, when a corporation may choose to move itself to wherever the tax code is most congenial, regardless of where its offices may sit, regulation is often difficult and contested. Google's corporate code of conduct famously included the injunction 'Don't be evil', and when it restructured into Alphabet, that adopted 'Do the right thing' as its motto. As it has become more widely crit-icised for everything from its tax avoidance policies to its tracking of users' activity, Google has often had these fine words thrown back at it as a rebuke, but the truth is that there is a corporate value to ethical conduct, over and above satisfying national regulations and consumer fads. In corruption-beset Nigeria, for example, Guaranty Trust Bank has risen to become one of the country's most profitable, precisely by seeking to adopt a strong ethical stance that sits in contrast – and some-times clashes with – local practices. It is not that there is not profit to be made from amorality and profiteering; rather, it is possible to do well by doing good, too.

Given that companies' successes and scandals, public messages and major officers' backgrounds are now all publicly available, this may help attract high-minded high-fliers, reas-sure investors worried about negative publicity over the horizon and woo the 'ethical customer'. With oil and gas conglomerate Shell vowing to produce net zero carbon by 2050, just to pick one of many examples, it seems that hard-nosed businesses are getting in touch with their inner moralist, even if only because this is the new way to sustainable profit.

This is something that can be harnessed also in addressing the new age of diversified conflict. Increasingly, these are fought within the realms of the private sector, whether duelling teams of lawyers and experts opining over the maritime boundaries in the Arctic or South China Sea, or the wildfire conflagrations of social media flame wars. Already, platforms such as Twitter and Facebook are – with varying degrees of enthusiasm – coming to accept they have responsibilities for the material they propagate. This is a start. There is also a growing market for what could be considered counter-weaponisation services and technologies. There are already companies marketing artificial intelligence and algorithm-driven systems able to identify and block or trace trolls and deceptive identities online. Some of these are, frankly, charlatans, but others are at the leading edge of this new arms race that may help make the online space less toxic and manipulative. By definition, the private sector tends to be more entrepreneurial, more imaginative, more nimble than the state. Just as it has been at the heart of so many of the problematic changes that are highlighted in this book, from the rise of the outsourced military contractor to the global supply chains that also ship guns, drugs and trafficked people, they can be part of the solution.

THE INDIVIDUAL: NEW RESPONSIBILITIES?

Finally, how far are we, as individual citizens, consumers and voters, more than just pawns and victims of the new world disorder? Just as autocrats would hope that their subjects love them, but will settle for their fear, apathy and hopelessness –

why rebel if there is no chance of getting anything better? – then so too the assumption that there is nothing we can do to change the world is the best way of ensuring we never do. In fact, there are three particular things we can all do to help make the world a better, safer place.

Click for it. It is all very well nodding sagely when someone suggests governments ought to support new media literacy and platforms ought to do more to block disinformation. The real vector for the spread of fake news, misleading memes and toxic narratives is us, retweeting articles we haven't really read, let alone considered, easily accepting news that fits our assumptions and agreeing with civility in principle, while gleefully feuding, vilifying and misrepresenting online in the specific. It is up to us to practise the kind of online ethics we would expect of others and be willing to withdraw our participation from those social media platforms that fail to play their part. It is relatively easy to support a Twitterstorm or call for a boycott in defence of our own rights and to protect those whom we like. The real challenge will be for us to do the same for those whose views and interests are not our own. The alternative is that we create communities which feel isolated and excluded, the perfect consumers of contrarian narratives and disruptive political agendas.

Work for it. The very technologies that leave us vulnerable to manipulation and subversion from the far corners of the world also allow us unprecedented opportunities to form communities for good. Online, we can amplify and help crowdfund initiatives that make the world a better place. Microcredit organisations such as Kiva and Lendwithcare provide small-scale development loans helping give people alternative, legitimate employment, saving some from drifting into the grip of insurgents, criminals and demagogues. Citizen journalism platforms mean that anyone with a smartphone camera, access or the time to commit can undermine the media-management techniques of governments and corporations. Organisations such as Bellingcat, blending professional investigative journalists, whistle-blowers and citizen journalists, have identified spies and uncovered atrocities.

Vote for it. Not all countries that call themselves democracies are truly democratic, but few are truly totalitarian. While there are huge differences in the opportunities between, say, the US, Russia (where there is still scope for local civil society, but not national opposition) and China (where the state seeks to dominate all political activity), in much of the world, the individual does have some scope to shape or at least influence their governments. There are brave people working for democracy or simply trying to make their voices heard in Russia and even China, and they need to be supported, encouraged and protected, when this is not going to be dangerous and counterproductive for them.

But those of us who can vote and campaign meaningfully ought meanwhile not to take that responsibility lightly. It may be glib to suggest that we get the politicians we deserve, but when we simply dismiss politics as the realm of the corrupt and the self-interested (which means we expect nothing better), when we are OK with our country adopting covert, zero-sum and coercive policies towards others and when we shrug and cast our ballots without expecting anything better, then we are in effect voting for the worst of the weaponised world.

CONCLUSIONS: OH BRAVE NEW WORLD

A book of this size cannot hope but sketch out the basic outlines of the potential new world of war and will be open to all kinds of critiques. And rightly so: while it is hard to argue against the notion that our individual, national and geopolitical environments are changing, quite what they are changing into is still very much open to debate. Indeed, that very act of debate in itself helps define the world.

This is one of the reasons why we have to consider our vocabulary. We will still have enemies and allies, but what these terms mean will change. Considering that Russia is meddling in Western politics and conducting high-tempo and often literally murderous intelligence operations within our boundaries, does that make it an enemy? And if so, why are we still buying Russian oil and gas, negotiating on arms control and encouraging oligarchs to bring their money here? Turkey is a member of NATO, an ally of the rest of the West. But if so, why is it threatening to unleash millions of migrants into Europe, buying Russian weaponry despite US concerns and backing jihadists in Syria and Libya alike? No simple definitions apply, and in effect everyone is simply on a spectrum of competitor, some shading into rival.

Likewise, outside explicitly military conflicts, notions of war and peace, victory and defeat become similarly hazy. There are victories, not *a* victory; there are escalations and de-escalations in the scale and seriousness of competition. There are also wholly new definitions of power. In conflicts of any kind, strength is dependent on having the appropriate tools for the job and the determination to employ them. If conflict is increasingly transferred to the realms of influence, connectivity, economic muscle and covert manipulation, then new indices of power will become more important. Once again to return to Stalin's question about how many divisions the Pope had, so long as the Papacy has spiritual authority, financial reserves and an intelligence capacity derived not from spies but from an extraordinary network of representatives, then maybe a handful of Swiss Guard in colourful costumes is enough? The Pope could, perhaps, ask how many social influencers Stalin had.

Arguably, this new world was ushered in by the collapse of the USSR, a classic example of a state that depended too much and for too long on military force, neglecting the soft power of ideology, the advantage of leading-edge technology or the fundamental necessity of a thriving economy. It was making the classic mistake of planning for the last war – the mass industrial clash against Hitler – rather than the next, the nimble political, technological and cultural one against democracy, computers and rock music.

Maybe it is fitting also to give the last word to Machiavelli: 'War should be the only study of a prince. He should consider peace only as a breathing-space, which gives him leisure to contrive, and furnishes the ability to execute military plans.' The Soviet leaders certainly considered 'peace only as a breathing-space' in their geopolitical struggle with the West, but failed in their study of war to see how it was changing. And since then, the pace of change has only accelerated, so it behoves us all, in the name of as much peace as we can contrive, to consider the new world of war, and whether we are ready for it, and have that many breathing-spaces of our own left.

WANT TO KNOW MORE?

For interesting takes on how life, politics, conflict and the world will evolve over the next few years and decades, I could recommend many, many works, but sadly will have to confine myself to a few that seem especially relevant: Christopher Coker's *Future*

War (Polity, 2015) on the nuts and bolts of man's inhumanity to man (and robots) and Robert Latiff's *Future War* (Vintage, 2018) for a more conceptual take, along with Andreas Krieg and Jean-Marc Rickli's *Surrogate Warfare: The Transformation of War in the Twenty-First Century* (Georgetown UP, 2019). For geopolitical shifts, Parag Khanna's *The Future Is Asian: Global Order in the Twenty-First Century* (Weidenfeld & Nicolson, 2019), Daniel Yergin's *The New Map: Energy, Climate, and the Clash of Nations* (Allen Lane, 2020) and Jennifer Welsh's *The Return of History: Conflict, Migration, and Geopolitics in the Twenty-First Century* (House of Anansi, 2016) are all worth a read, albeit for very different reasons. For a very big picture, Adrian Hon's *A New History of the Future in 100 Objects: A Fiction* (MIT Press, 2020) is an upbeat and humane perspective, while Andrew Maynard's *Future Rising: A Journey from the Past to the Edge of Tomorrow* (Mango, 2020) is as much manifesto as projection.

Index

Index

Bellingcat, 18, 19, 222
Belt and Road Initiative, 58, 82–4, 133
Benin, 50
Biden, Joseph, 81
Bin Laden, Osama, 109
Bin Salman, Prince Mohammed, 59–60, 172
biological warfare, 89, 130, 163–4
Blackwill, Robert, 85
Bolsonaro, Jair, 118
Bolton, Giles, 144
Bolton, John, 128–9
Bond, James, 60, 176, 186
'borelords', 36–7, 156
Bos, Daniel, 191
boycotts, 19, 68, 221
branding, national, 17, 177–9
Brazil, 118
Brexit, 148, 161, 167, 217
British East India Company, 48
Brooking, Emerson, 175
Browder, Bill, 150
Bulgaria, 106, 164, 181
Bull, Hedley, 13–14
Bullough, Oliver, 101
Burgis, Tom, 101
Burundi, 133
Byzantium, 35

Cambodia, 118
Canada, 119, 128, 197
Caribbean, 48
Castro, Fidel, 105
Central African Republic, 78, 133
Chagos Islands, 52–3
Chayes, Sarah, 101
Chechnya, 30, 116–17
chemical weapons, 13, 210–11
Chile, 73

China, People's Republic, 3–4, 16, 37, 58, 80–1, 89–90, 96, 98, 117, 118, 119, 133, 150, 182–4, 199, 212–13, 222
and Africa, 45, 58, 82, 171
censorship, 68, 183, 222
and COVID-19, 140–1, 164, 183–4, 205
cultural statecraft, 176–7, 179, 182–4
economic statecraft, 67–9, 80–1, 82–4, 86, 87–90, 94–5, 100, 119, 133, 134
espionage, 114–15, 119, 203–4
information operations and media, 164, 169–71, 176–7
and international institutions, 212–13
military deployments and bases abroad, 45, 49, 53, 58
and South China Sea, 151–3
see also Belt and Road Initiative; Huawei
China, Republic of, 67–8, 84, 117, 140, 151, 171, 183
Chinkin, Christine, 43
Chua, Amy, 206
Churchill, Winston, 168
CIA, 105, 131, 169, 179, 181
climate change, 134–5, 204, 216, 219–20
Clinton, Hillary, 160, 162, 168
Cockayne, James, 123
coercive diplomacy, 11, 51–2
COIN, 157–8
Coker, Christopher, 224–5
Cold War, 19, 42–3, 71, 131–2, 134, 163–4, 178, 186, 198, 205
Colombia, 108, 127, 128, 133, 140

Index

Index

Index

Index

Index

Obama, Barack, 155, 213
Obermayer, Frederik and
    Bastian, 101
oil, 86, 99
open source intelligence and
    citizen journalism, 18, 221–2
Organisation for the Prohibition
    of Chemical Weapons,
    210–11
O'Sullivan, Meghan, 85

Pakistan, 39–40, 41–2, 54, 84,
    110, 133, 134, 135
Palau, 67–9, 100, 140
Palestinians, 147
Palmer, Andrew, 63
Panama, 105
pandas, weaponisation of, 3–4,
    141
Paoli, Letizia, 122
Papacy, 13, 16–17, 25–6, 34, 69,
    208, 223–4
Paracel Islands, 152
Patrikarakos, David, 175
peace treaties, 35
peacekeeping, 49, 53–4
Philippines, 118, 151, 153
Pinker, Steven, 39
piracy, 44–5, 48–9, 70, 120
Poland, 35, 216
policing, 120–2, 157
political war, 12, 51, 166–9,
    201–4
Pomerantsev, Peter, 175
Pooh, Winnie-the-, 93
Prigozhin, Evgeny, 56, 165–6
private military companies see
    mercenaries
psychological warfare, 11–12
Putin, Vladimir, 7–8, 30, 41, 74,
    148, 167, 186, 214

Qatar, 162, 163

rare earths, 86
red mercury, 109–10
reflexive control, 93–4
religion, 14, 33–4, 35, 40, 41–2,
    177
Ren Zhengfei, 86, 89, 92
Renaissance, 14–17, 18, 57, 104–5,
    119–20, 130, 207–8, 210
resilience, 98–100, 219–20
Responsibility to Protect (R2P),
    38
Rickli, Jean-Marc, 209, 225
Rid, Thomas, 20, 175
Robinson, Linda, 20
Roman Empire, 33–4, 69, 84,
    177–8
RT, 169–70
Russell, William Howard, 31
Russia, 4, 30–1, 35, 37, 41, 49,
    51, 55–6, 57–8, 62, 72, 79,
    80, 81, 91–2, 108–9, 120,
    135, 136, 145–6, 148–9, 150,
    155–6, 165–9, 185–8, 189,
    196, 210–11, 214, 215, 222
    and Africa, 45, 55
    and Arctic, 147, 153–4
    and Asia, 213
    economic statecraft, 98, 99,
        136–7
    espionage, 102–4, 203–4, 211,
        223 see also FSB; GRU; SVR
    and Europe, 90–1, 94
    and Latin America, 55
    media, 169–70
    military deployments and
        exercises, 45, 46, 49, 55–6,
        187–8
    political war, 93–4, 165–9,
        170

232

Index

Russian communities abroad, 103, 120, 154–5
and the West, 52
see also Crimea; Donbas; wars, Syrian
Rwanda, 38, 54, 57, 138

Safieddine, Fadi, 174
sanctions, 69–81, 93–4, 141
economic, 69–81
and Iran, 75–6, 155
and North Korea, 77–8
personal, 77, 156–7, 165
and Russia, 73–4, 77, 79
Sarkozy, Nicolas, 95
Sassanids, 35
Saudi Arabia, 28, 40, 54, 59–60, 61–2, 92, 95–6, 109–10, 149, 172, 189, 217
Schröder, Gerhard, 90–1
Scotland, 35, 146, 167
Serbia, 138, 139
Shanghai Cooperation Organisation, 213
Sierra Leone, 84, 107
Simonyan, Margarita, 170
Singapore, 216
signalling, 187–9
Singer, P.W., 63, 175
Snow, Nancy, 191
Snowden, Edward, 61
social media, 3, 161–3, 172–4, 218–20
see also Facebook; information warfare, trolls; TikTok; Twitter; Vkontakte; YouTube
soft power, 17, 50–1, 218
'soldiering-plus', 45–52
Somalia, 29, 42, 44–5, 120, 133, 142

South Africa, 73, 217
South China Sea, 49, 147, 151–3, 220
South Sudan, 90–1, 133
Soviet Union, 14, 29–30, 71–2, 82, 103, 105–6, 131–2, 134, 154, 163–4, 178, 223–4
space, 16, 53, 147
Spain, 46, 62, 140, 167
sport, weaponisation of, 5, 41, 73, 169, 178, 182–3, 186
Sri Lanka, 83
Strachan, Hew, 43
Stalin, Joseph, 71, 131, 223–4
Sudan, 58
Sun Tzu, 20
SVR (Foreign Intelligence Service), 104, 113, 203
Sweden, 187, 204, 217, 218
SWIFT, 79–80
Switzerland, 210
Syria, 30, 32, 40, 41, 55–6, 72, 115–16, 133, 135–6, 138–9, 141, 145–6, 185, 223

Taiwan *see* China, Republic of
Tajikistan, 133
Tanzania, 133
telecommunications industry, 86–90, 212
terrorism, 4, 29, 42, 50–1, 60–1, 105–6, 108, 109, 120, 188–9, 199
Thomson, Andrew, 63
Tibet, 95, 183
TikTok, 3
Tilly, Charles, 119–20
tourism, 67–9
Transnistria, 120, 155
Transparency International, 90–1

233

Index

Index